KEYS TO
UNDERSTANDING

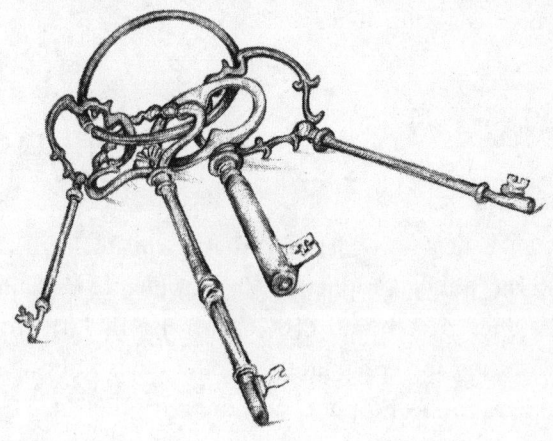

Endorsements

John and Caryl are one of those couples Hebrews 13:7 refers to when it says, "Whose faith follow." You can look at their pathway and find a compass for following Jesus with intimate abandonment. Their story will both inspire and confirm your own journey in Christ.

Bob Sorge
Author of *Power Of The Blood*

Paul instructs all believers to desire earnestly spiritual gifts, especially and preeminently the gift of prophecy. Why prophecy? Because the one who prophesies edifies the church (1 Corinthians 14:1,4). You will be blessed by John's inspiring and entertaining account of his and Caryl's journey along the road of learning to prophesy and mentor others.

Dr. Wes Adams
Co-Author and Editor of *Life in the Spirit Study Bible*

Some people have a message and others become the message. John and Caryl O'Shaughnessy live the testimony of Jesus. We watched them raise their children in Kansas City fully pursuing God every day of their lives. They lived the spirit of prophecy until their family became the testimony of Jesus. You need this book, you need this testimony, you need to become the message!

Kirk Bennett, Director of ZHOP
Zadok House of Prayer, Charlotte, North Carolina

In the culture we live in, John and Caryl's story is unique. They are both passionate followers of Jesus Christ who take their gifts of prayer, prophecy, and encouraging others seriously. They are forerunners who have had their mettle tested. John and Caryl model living for God even when the cost is high and the future uncertain. The O'Shaughnessys' faith journey and life of obedience inspires us and has led the way for countless others to follow.

Tim & Anne Evans
Real Life Ministries, Colorado Springs, Colorado

Out here in the West, I'd describe John and Caryl with the simple words: "They're the real deal." They walk their talk and are both inspirational and down-to-earth at the same time. It's been my privilege to be encouraged by them over the years, and I trust you will be encouraged by these words as well.

David Warnick, Executive Pastor
New Life Community Church, Rathdrum, Idaho

John and Caryl O'Shaughnessy are authentic, loving, real, and sincere. They are refreshingly passionate in their commitment to Christ without any religious aftertaste. They are committed to hearing God and the prophetic, but wise to potential pitfalls and excess. They have been good friends in our lives for the past fifteen years. We got to know them at the Elgin Vineyard before becoming head pastors there. We recommend their friendship, counsel, and ministry.

Tom & Jill Severson, Pastor
Elgin Vineyard Christian Fellowship, Elgin, Illinois

KEYS TO UNDERSTANDING

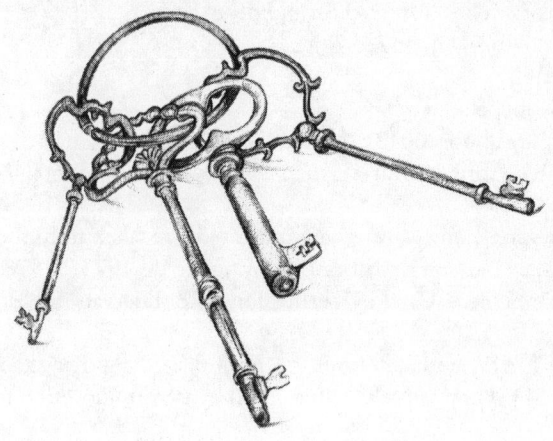

JOHN O'SHAUGHNESSY

ELGIN, ILLINOIS

Keys to Understanding by John O'Shaughnessy

Copyright © 2009 by John O'Shaughnessy. All rights reserved.
No part of this book may reproduced in any form without permission of the author. However, the reader is welcome to quote brief passages for purposes of review.

Cover design: Brendan O'Shaughnessy
Cover and text art sketches: Caryl O'Shaughnessy
Book layout: Mary Anne Pfitzinger

Published by This Joy! Books
P.O. Box 823, Elgin, Illinois 60121, www.thisjoybooks.com
A Division of Three Cord Ministries, Inc., Libertyville, Illinois 60048

All Scripture quotations, unless otherwise indicated, are taken from the *Holy Bible*, New International Version®. NIV®. Copyright © 1973, 1978, 1984 by International Bible Society. Used by permission of Zondervan Publishing House. All rights reserved.
Scripture marked NKJV are taken from the *Holy Bible*, New King James Version. Copyright © 1982 by Thomas Nelson, Inc. Used by permission. All rights reserved.

ISBN-13: 978-0-9821835-3-3
First printing, 2009. Printed in the United States of America

*To my wife, Caryl,
who is my ministry partner and my best friend,
and to our children, LeAnn, Erin, and Brendan.*

*This book is also dedicated to everyone
at Metro Christian Fellowship
and the International House of Prayer
in Kansas City, Missouri, who helped us along our journey.
Holy treasures have been deposited in me
and vision has been imparted to me
by the godly men and women who have encouraged us as a family
to carefully examine God's truth, to pursue Him at all times
regardless of the costs, and to behold the beauty of the Lord.*

Table of Contents

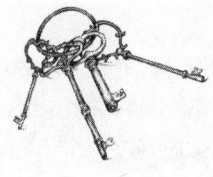

	Foreword	x
	Preface	xii
	Acknowledgements	xv
Chapter 1	Are You Talking to Me?	1
Chapter 2	God's Promise to Caryl	11
Chapter 3	A Living Prophetic Word	15
Chapter 4	Change	19
Chapter 5	Our First Prophetic Conference	23
Chapter 6	More Change	33
Chapter 7	Moving On	37
Chapter 8	Wind of the Spirit	45
Chapter 9	Our New Duplex	49
Chapter 10	A New Season	55
Chapter 11	Prophetic Training: In the School of Humility	61
Chapter 12	Stepping up the Ladder	71
Chapter 13	Another Demotion?	77
Chapter 14	Praiseworthy Painting	83
Chapter 15	A Word of Caution	89
Chapter 16	Blessings As a Result of Obedience	91
Chapter 17	Forerunners	97
	Afterword	107
	Appendix	109

Foreword

IT HAS BEEN MY JOY AND HONOR to know the O'Shaughnessy family for fifteen years. I remember when this "wet behind the ears" family moved to the KC area forsaking all they knew to come into the land of the prophetic in Kansas City. Boy, did they know what they were getting into . . . not!

Before I go any further, let's make the playing field level—none of us has many clues. But we are all on a search looking for the City and its builder and architect who is God Himself. We are all on a pilgrimage together to become. Yes, we are all on a path less walked upon in the process of becoming more like our Master and Lover of our Souls—Jesus.

In fact, that is what this book you have in your hands is all about. *Keys to Understanding* is more than the next how-to book from the latest prophetic star rising on the scene. This book is a story filled with hope, faith, and love; it's about a family on a journey pursuing their destiny together in life. You see, John and Caryl have learned that gifts are gifts—they are given. But character grows in the field of His love.

Wow! This is really a true-to-life read! Consider topics like—The School of Humility, Another Demotion?, Living a Prophetic Word. . . . This is wonderful! I would rather walk with ten people who *live* a word than one hundred who can give a word. Now to make sure I am not misunderstood, I am not down on the prophetic. I love it. I incite. I encourage it. I am it!

But how refreshing it is for God to use a businessman and an artsy gal to dump His good ole gifts upon and turn them into prophetic equippers. Now that I love! *Keys to Understanding* is a gentle and humble manual about living a life surrendered to the lordship of Jesus Christ and learning to love His people by releasing the power of His presence and His gifts.

It has been the honor of Michal Ann and me to walk with this dear couple for many years. While Michal Ann has now graduated to her heavenly reward, I just cannot help but think that she is smiling as I compile this foreword for this dear couple's first book. Not only did our kids stay all night with them on many occasions, but even our two dogs had a wedding ceremony at their house one time. So we are sort of related!

So blessings to each of you as you partake of the life shared in these transparent pages. Perhaps you, too, will be so caught up in the presence and purposes of God that you will fall head over heels in love with the One who captured John and Caryl's heart. After all, the journey is all about Him.

When you read this book, you will love God even more!

Because He lives!

James W. Goll
Encounters Network, Prayer Storm, Compassion Acts
Franklin, Tennessee

Preface

THE NOTION THAT GOD ACTUALLY TALKS to people may seem a bit odd to you. It did to me. I never knew that God desired direct communication with His people. I thought that He had too many things on His mind to be thinking about me and my situations. The question that needs to be asked isn't, does God speak? but rather, Are you listening when God is talking?

Why wouldn't God talk to regular, ordinary people on a variety of subjects? Wouldn't God want to communicate with us? Don't loving fathers naturally want to talk to their children? In our family, communication is essential. It's really no different in our heavenly family, but I never knew that God desperately wanted to talk to me. Hearing His voice is my part in an ongoing and active journey that began when I was about thirty-four years old. One of my life messages is that if God can talk to me, He can talk to you, too.

The word prophecy puts off some people. Some think prophecy is reserved for super mystics or the specially gifted. Another common misconception is that hearing God's voice is reserved for those who are mature either spiritually or in age. The truth is that God wants all to prophesy (see 1 Corinthians 14).

My wife, Caryl, and I are ordinary people. Caryl went to art school and I was a businessman. We were not trained in a seminary. Most of our education for ministry came through the "School of Hard Knocks." For some unknown reason, God has chosen us to encourage others to listen to Him.

Starting a ministry, especially a prophetic ministry, was the last thing on our minds. We are not professional ministers. I have never been accused of having lots of pulpit savvy! We are weak and broken, and God in His goodness was showing His supreme sense of humor by depositing within me, of all people, a prophetic gift. I connect with Moses in Exodus 4:10 when he says,

O LORD, I have never been eloquent, neither in the past nor since you have spoken to your servant. I am slow of speech and tongue (Exodus 4:10 *The Full Life Study Bible,* New International Version).

As a child growing up, I stuttered constantly. Not a day went by that I didn't stutter through almost every sentence. From first grade until I graduated from eighth grade, I took private speech lessons three times a week. My speech teacher was a wonderful woman who inspired me in countless ways. Without her ability to see past my stuttering, who knows how my life would have turned out? She was an inspiration to me.

In February of 2002, thirty years after my last speech lesson, I had a desire to contact her. I had no idea where she lived or if she was still living. I wasn't even sure if she would remember me. I wanted to reconnect with her and let her know the impact she'd had upon my life. I had often thought about her; I'd written college papers about her and even told my children about her. After an Internet search, I found five people in Illinois with the same last name. I wrote a generic letter to all five asking if they knew of a speech pathologist that taught at my grade school in the mid-sixties. Much to my surprise, her daughter e-mailed me and said that I was trying to track down her mother. My former teacher wrote to me and said that she remembered me immediately. I then wrote a simple letter expressing my gratitude to her for the long hours she'd spent working with me.

To sum up, God selected me, a shy person who was slow of speech, a man who knew nothing about prophecy, one who attended an evangelical church where prophecy was not taught or experienced. Without warning or explanation, God invaded time and space and totally disrupted my life with the gift of prophecy.

Actually my story is really our family story. The truth is that Caryl and I wrote the book together. It's a collaboration all the way through; I didn't do it by myself. In many ways, our family is just like yours or the one next door. I hope that in reading this book you'll see how our journey might be like yours.

Another reason for writing is to do my part to clear up deceptions and misunderstandings about the gift of prophecy that exist both inside and outside the church. Misunderstanding and deception bothers me. I'm sure they grieve God.

There may be some who picked up this book who have had negative experiences with the prophetic or a prophetic word given to them and have decided that it is no longer worth pursuing. I hope that reading our story may encourage you to reconsider your position. I have met hundreds of people over the past fifteen years who have become disinterested in prophecy and in hearing God's voice. I pray that this book will encourage you, even in a small way, to continue to listen for the voice of God and to see how prophecy, when exercised within God-given boundaries, can change a person, a family, a church, or even a nation.

Have you ever heard God's voice before? You probably have but did not recognize that He was speaking to you. I exhort you to start listening for Him. I guarantee it will change your life. I hope this book will start you on that quest. Hearing God's voice is not the finish line. It only represents part of your journey to draw closer to Him. Listening and obeying Him will ultimately draw you closer to Him. And as God talks to you about yourself and about other people He wants you to encourage and comfort, they too will be drawn closer to our Savior.

I encourage the reader to have an open heart and a teachable spirit when reading this simple book. God has given me many surprises over the years. He has wonderful surprises waiting for you as well.

John O'Shaughnessy

Acknowledgements

NEVER IN MY WILDEST DREAMS did I ever imagine writing a book. At first, I wasn't even sure I had a story to tell. As I started to write, I needed all the help that Caryl and our children could give me. They read the manuscript and remembered stories and events I had forgotten. Then our friend, Ginny Emery, volunteered to read our manuscript. God used her to breathe life into my run-on sentences. Her husband, Ed, graciously allowed Ginny to spend hours tweaking our feeble attempts to tell our story. Thanks, Ed and Ginny.

Many people played an essential part in our journey. A few filled such key roles at strategic points in my life that I must honor them.

- Jim and Joyce Gochenour led the prophetic nurture group in Kansas City that was a springboard into our itinerant prophetic ministry.

- Jim and Michal Ann Goll saw potential in us that we were unable to see ourselves. Their friendship was just as valuable as their mentoring.

- Even when we were young and inexperienced, our financial supporters invested in what seemed like a high-risk Kingdom venture. We could not have made it this far without you.

ONE

Are You Talking to Me?

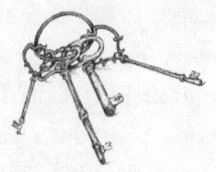

WE HAD A GREAT MARRIAGE. I had a fantastic job. Why did we feel something was missing? But it was; something was missing between God and us. So, my wife, Caryl, and I were reevaluating everything. At the time we had three young, healthy children, LeAnn, Erin, and John Brendan. We loved spending time at home; we loved playing with our children, taking them to the park or going on family vacations. In some ways, we were living the American Dream. I had a great wife, great kids, a great church, and a great job. We sensed something growing between us and God, and we wanted to go deeper. We wanted more. We did not know exactly what that meant or how we would go about it. We knew that Caryl's lifelong desire to learn and experience more in prayer was part of it. That's the launching pad for our story.

Our year of transition began in 1992. First, we began feeling like we wanted to look for a new church. It is hard to find language to express what was going on inside; even now about all I can say is that Caryl and I both had a funny feeling that we were being challenged to walk in faith.

We were hungry. In fact, Caryl had been praying for many years for this hunger to be filled and for the Holy Spirit to express Himself more fully through our lives. We felt like we were setting out on a quest and finding more of God was the treasure we needed to search for. We didn't know that God was getting ready to move us.

Our good friends, Doug and Kathy Neal, lived several towns away. We had known them from our church, but we had lost touch with them for a while because Doug was fully occupied finishing an advanced degree in psychology. He called one day to tell me they had just moved to our town, a pleasant suburb northwest of Chicago. It was so good to hear his voice again. We reminisced a bit. When he mentioned that he needed help unloading furniture from the moving truck, I gladly helped him. As time went on, we saw the Neals much more. Sometimes I'd drive over and talk with Doug, and other times we'd get together as couples. Caryl and I connected with them right from the start. It's hard to describe, but there was chemistry, a kindred spirit between us. God knit our lives together in a wonderful manner. We could talk to them about anything at anytime. They were the kind of friends we could call at three in the morning if we needed help. They impacted our lives in countless positive ways. When we would get together, it was typical to end the night praying for each other. The Neals were walking with us in our search for more intimacy with God. They were ahead of us but gladly invited us along. We loved to listen to them talk about their faith in God.

One particular night, as we were all sharing, Caryl and I expressed a desire to know God more and to take whatever measures were necessary to pursue Him. We asked the Neals to pray for us. We wanted God and His plans and purposes. As they prayed, something began to happen inside of me. For some unknown reason, it was different from the other times they prayed for us. Caryl still remembers feeling the Holy Spirit that evening as the Neals prayed. Looking back, we now realize that we were being launched and commissioned through the Holy Spirit for a plan not yet revealed. The Lord has plans to position us all, plans to commission us for strategic spots as we choose to say, "YES, Lord, send me."

Several weeks later, Doug asked if Caryl and I had any plans for New Year's Eve, which was a few weeks away. "What did you and Kathy have in mind?" I asked. "The Evanston Vineyard is having a New Year's Eve celebration service and we wanted to invite you." *You mean, you're going to spend New Year's Eve at church?* I thought to myself. Something about Doug's invitation intrigued me. Immediately I said yes. This was out of the ordinary because I always checked with Caryl before making plans, especially for New Year's Eve. But this time something was different. I wasn't sure why, but this invitation was one I had to accept.

As the weeks passed, I actually found myself looking forward to the New Year's Eve service at the Evanston Vineyard. I was even more thrilled when I found out that the dress code for the evening was casual attire. At the time, I worked in sales and wore a suit and tie to work. I used to jokingly call it my "uniform." Once I came home, I would immediately change into casual clothes.

The night finally arrived, December 31, 1992. During the hour drive to the church, Doug explained to us that the service would be different, not like anything we were used to. When we arrived, I noticed we were among the oldest people there, and I was only thirty-four years old. Most of the people in attendance were college students or young adults. The service was filled with singing, dancing, testimonies, and prayer. Although it was a marked difference from what we were accustomed to, Caryl and I felt the differences were quite refreshing. During the worship time, I found myself meditating on God and His majesty instead of merely mouthing the words and looking around at the people near me. The words and melodies were touching my heart in an unusual way.

Near the end of the service, four men and a woman approached the front of the church and took their places near the microphone. At first I thought they were going to play a second set of worship songs. They looked like either pastors or elders from the church. One by one, they began speaking to various people in the church. We did not know what was happening, but later it was explained to us that they were a prophetic team ministering to people. As the pastors began sharing certain things with people in the congregation, these people would break down and start crying. I wondered what was happening inside them. In my view, these leaders were merely talking to the people. *What was causing them to cry like that?* The impact these words were having on people made a profound impression on me. This happened three or four times and each time the person on the receiving end would start sobbing, sometimes uncontrollably. I was a bit confused about what was going on, but being a visitor, I kept quiet and watched. Whatever these pastors were saying seemed to reflect Christ's love for the people and encouraged and comforted them.

Every so often I would look at the lead pastor and it seemed like he was staring at me. This happened several times. Each time our eyes came close to locking on each other, I quickly glanced away. At some point my mind began to fade or daydream because it was getting late. I wasn't really concentrating on what was being said from the front when it happened. The lead pastor, who was part of the group of five, said, "There is a married couple in the fourth row and the man has a blue sweater on. Could you please stand up?" I looked at Caryl and softly whispered without turning my head, "He's talking to us!" I was fairly confident he had us mixed up with another couple because we had never met this man, and I was quite sure he did not know us. As we stood to our feet I held Caryl's hand tightly. I remember having a smirk on my face because I was sure that once we stood up and he could see us better, he would realize his mistake and recognize that he had picked the wrong couple. I was quite confident he had us mixed up with someone who looked like us. He looked at us and calmly and lovingly said, "You have been banging your heads up against a barrier or a ceiling. You are dissatisfied, asking yourselves, 'What's next?' You are on the crest of a fresh wave. The Lord is in all of this. He's releasing new work which will make your heart burn."

Wow! What in the world was going on?! As soon as the pastor began speaking these things, I felt a warmth that started on the top of my head and slowly worked its way down to my feet. It took a while and seemed strange to me at the time. I had never felt anything like this before. My smirk vanished! My attention was now riveted on what was being said.

To tell the truth, we were dissatisfied. We looked like happy evangelicals in one of the largest growing churches on the planet. We'd been baptized there as adults; all our children had been dedicated there, and we'd gladly served—in small group ministry, loving every minute of it! We had planned to spend our whole lives there. We had grown up in neighboring communities, and all our friends and family lived nearby. But in the midst of everything positive, it felt like we'd reached a ceiling and that we were, in a sense, banging our heads against it. On one level things were going great at church. We loved and supported our leaders and loved everything about the place. We were growing spiritually and serving in various capacities. But something was missing, and we didn't know what it was. Caryl had always had a desire to grow in the area of prayer but wasn't exactly sure how to nurture it. We both wanted a deeper relationship with the Lord. Of course our church had outlets for those desires but for some unique reason, we were coming up empty and wanting more.

The pastor continued, "The Lord has built a solid foundation in your personal and married life. You have had much service and ministry experience. You have tremendous potential." Somewhere in the midst of that last sentence my body went numb! *Who was this man? And more importantly, how did he know those intimate details of OUR lives?* In hindsight, it seemed as if he knew too much about us and about our circumstances. Just then it hit me. I thought my friend Doug had talked with the pastor before the service and asked if maybe the pastor could help us somehow. *After all, isn't that what pastors do?*

That pastor was right! Our personal lives had solid spiritual foundations. Both of us had been raised in great, nurturing, God-fearing homes. Like many other young couples we knew at church, I sensed that some day we would be in ministry together. I had no idea when, who, what, where, or why. The details were not clear and we were not in a hurry to try to make anything happen on our own.

KEYS TO UNDERSTANDING

We had been married almost thirteen years, and we had a great marriage. It was routine when the kids were small to put them to bed and then to spend the next hour or two talking together. We talked about everything! Caryl loved it and I loved it. Frankly, there was always something we could find to talk about. I loved being with Caryl and spending time with her. She is a perfect match for my personality.

The pastor then paused, looked at Caryl, and continued, "Listen to things. You've discounted things because they have been too far out. He is speaking to you. Listen to Him. It's not too weird." Another pastor said to me, "Listen to her (meaning Caryl), she has something to say." He smiled at us and said we could sit down. I sat down and felt my knees weaken. *What in the world just happened? And what was causing me to feel so warm all over?* Surely I wasn't coming down with a fever. Again I asked myself two questions. First, "What is this 'thing' called?" Second, "How did he know all those details about us?" This man just told me the secret desires of my heart. It felt both wonderful and intrusive. *How did he do that? He didn't know me! How could that be? Is this Biblical?*

December 31, 1992 was the last day I remember living a normal, predictable, and uneventful life. God supernaturally intervened in our lives that evening. I felt like Paul after his Damascus Road experience. God had begun a process that changed us forever. The process continues to unfold, both in ministry and as a family.

We left the New Year's Eve service a bit tired, definitely encouraged, and yet puzzled. We pulled into our driveway about 1:45 AM and quickly went to bed. I awoke the next morning, and everything seemed remarkably different. The realization that someone I knew might go to hell suddenly overwhelmed me. As I looked out the window and watched a man shovel a driveway, I began crying uncontrollably. I prayed like never before for his salvation. Our three children and Caryl looked at me and asked me what was wrong. I said, "People are going to hell and don't even know it. We need to tell them about Jesus." In an instant I felt God's heart. I wasn't sure why, but I did. I was surprised by my new emotions. I wondered why I hadn't felt this urgency about someone's salvation before.

Was I having an early midlife crisis at thirty-four years old? I don't know how it happened, but I became a worshipper overnight. It was as if all the head knowledge I had about God suddenly found its way to my heart. When this took place, my heart exploded. In addition, I had an appetite to read the Word of God that was greater than any I'd ever had before. Bible reading was a part of my normal routine, but somehow this immediately intensified. I loved reading the Word, but I was not disciplined to read it every day. Suddenly, I began waking up early and reading my Bible for several hours before starting my forty-five minute commute to work. I knew something was happening in my life, but I could not explain it to anybody. It seemed that Caryl's prayers for me these last seven years were being answered all at once and in strange ways.

For example, as a young Christian, I had always been a closet cigarette smoker. I'd tried stopping a hundred times and each time I'd failed miserably. I also enjoyed drinking beer from time to time. This changed overnight. After the New Year's Eve service, my desire for cigarettes and beer left immediately. I couldn't figure it out at first, but the desire simply left me. I guess God did a miracle so He could be glorified.

Several days later, I was meeting with Doug at 6:00 AM to pray. We were not only friends but also prayer partners. We met at his office to pray on a regular basis. After a few moments of small talk, we started to pray for each other. I immediately began seeing pictures in my mind. Later I found out they were called visions. They're described in the Bible. I simply knew certain things about Doug that had never crossed my mind before. For example, all of a sudden I knew that Doug's lease was almost up on his office space and that his current landlord was going to increase the rent significantly if he decided to sign another lease.

When I told Doug, he asked, "Did Kathy tell you?" I said "no," yet I wasn't sure how I knew that detail of a very specific situation about Doug's business. After several similar interactions, I said rather boldly to Doug, "There is another office God has reserved for you. It is near a set of railroad tracks. It is a two-story building with brick trim and there is white trim near the top."

KEYS TO UNDERSTANDING

I returned home at around seven that morning and told Caryl what happened at Doug's office. We weren't sure what to make of it, and I needed to drive to work, so I left quickly. As a salesman, I routinely had plenty of time to myself in the car during the daily commute. As my mind was busily trying to figure out exactly what was going on, I enjoyed feeling God's affirmation over my life. I was awakened to the fact that God was enjoying me in my immaturity. This was a new concept. *Why would God be enjoying me in these new experiences?* This sense of His enjoyment continues to unfold the longer we are in ministry.

In Mike Bickle's book, *The Pleasures of Loving God,* he writes,

I am loved, and I am a lover. I can be confident in the fact that God loves me in my immaturity, and in my immaturity, I return my love back to Him. Along with that, because I am loved and I am a lover, I am successful in my humanity as a person during my time on the earth. My primary success is because of that one spiritual principle and fact: I am loved, and I am a lover of God. No matter what else happens, in the most profound way, I am already successful because I have received His free love and have become a follower of Jesus (Lake Mary, Florida: Creation House, 2000).

The rest of the week was filled with more surprises—surprises that included knowing detailed facts about certain about people when I looked at them. Some were complete strangers who I met at the gas station or grocery store. Some were people I knew. Other times I knew who was going to call on the telephone before the phone rang. I was careful not to share these surprisingly new and fresh encounters with anyone except Caryl. This went on for several months. These revelation experiences continued and increased. Not only was I knowing things about people and having visions, but I was also having strange dreams.

Before long I began hearing a voice on the inside of me. (Later I heard people describe this as the internal, audible voice of God.) When I told Doug about all this he seemed to know it was the gift of prophecy. *The gift of what?* I thought to myself. I knew nothing about prophecy—other than the fact I could spell it. I reasoned with myself that since I had received no teaching on prophecy during all those years of going to church, somehow God had picked the wrong guy. *Surely I wasn't supposed to be given the gift of prophecy. Why would God give someone a spiritual gift that they didn't believe in? How could He give a gift to someone without teaching or previous exposure to it?*

Caryl, on the other hand, was thrilled because she had been praying for seven years that the Holy Spirit would lead our family through me. She saw God moving in my life and in our situation. In fact, God had begun speaking to her about me the first night we met on February 6, 1976. Let me have Caryl tell you the story.

TWO

God's Promise to Caryl
(As Told by Caryl)

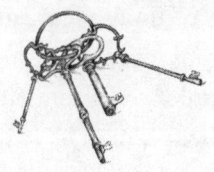

I LOVE TO TELL THE STORY of how John and I first met. It's not only significant because we ended up getting married, but it was also a definite mile marker in my life, one that foretold God's destiny for us.

Let me give you some background. I grew up in a Christian family. At the age of five, with my parents' help, I dedicated my life to Jesus. I always remember being a Christian. It was a natural transition for me because from an early age, my mom prayed with me. As a young child, I knew the magnificent presence of the Lord. Later as an adult, I heard my childhood experience described as "entering into His sanctuary of communion." While I was still a little girl, my mom and I began praying regularly for a Christian husband, a man specially selected for me by God. Some twelve years later God not only answered our early prayers, but He also began to show me that He had designed a far bigger plan for me than I had asked for, one that is still unfolding.

KEYS TO UNDERSTANDING

As a senior in high school, I was longing for Christian friends, even for just one. It was a lonely season being a believer with unbelieving friends. None of my school friends were believers. One evening, the night before a family ski vacation, I was at the house of my closest friend from school. She was going to watch my dog while we were on vacation. Without expecting anything special to happen this cold February night, I unexpectedly received an invitation from God. His invitation was the starting point of divine initiatives made by a creative God who loves to lavish gifts on His children. I'll try my best to describe it.

We were just hanging out together, watching the 1976 Winter Olympics on television. It was one of those teen gatherings with lots of energy and noise. Later in the evening, two young men came in. One of them was John. Before I was even introduced to him, the Holy Spirit spoke some beautiful things to my heart about him. The Holy Spirit didn't quite speak in words, but in a strong knowing, that God had selected John for a ministry that would affect thousands. I knew that it wasn't just a ministry to unknown people, but that there was a generational blessing as well. I was amazed, sensing that somehow, in some way, many of these dear people would be family to me as well. "Wow," I thought, "Could this possibly be my future husband? Is he the answer to my prayers?" I felt like I had received a heavenly invitation—I knew this invitation was for me, an opportunity to grasp what God had planned for my life, but I also knew that it would be about John, too.

This was so exciting to me. Could this be the friend I was longing for? I was overwhelmed with joy, knowing that the Lord had just shown me that He had a call for both my life and for John's. As the night went on, I was eventually introduced to John. For me, it was love at first sight, a different kind of instant love. The Lord dropped His heart for John into mine. But I kept this to myself. I didn't realize that John was a half-hearted believer; he had not completely given his life over to Jesus. Only later, when we talked about our faith, did I learn of the gaps that existed between my faith and his.

That night, God not only showed me something about His plan for us, He also gave me my first official assignment as an intercessor, the job of being a prayer warrior for John. So I immediately began to pray for him and our future and the ministry He had for us.

Our relationship began to grow that night. It continued when John went off to the Marines in San Diego, California, for three years. Although we were miles apart, we remained close. Four years after we met, while John was in college at Illinois State University and I was living at home, attending the American Academy of Art near Chicago, John gave his life to the Lord. He came to faith through a friend who was part of a college-based ministry called the Navigators. The first thing he did after meeting Jesus was to call me on the phone. He knew that I had been praying since we met for him to have a personal relationship with God—and praying for a Christian husband since I was a child! John knew if he gave his life to the Lord he could marry me. That had been clearly communicated through many discussions. John could not fake it. It had to be real.

A year later, on August 8, 1980, we were married. As you can imagine, I was thrilled and thanked God for answering my childhood prayers for a Christian husband. Even though God had given me faith for John and set me praying for him on the night we met, my faith had been tested and my prayer life exercised and stretched by many challenges in the four years before our wedding day. By the time we exchanged vows, I sensed that our marriage was God's good plan and purpose. He had put me on this path that February night when He sent John into my life. I am grateful that the Lord has led me so graciously.

I felt John and I were made for one another, that we were God's first pick for each other, His ultimate best. **God wants to direct us in all areas of our lives**. It sure is fun when we are in tune with His voice. If I had not believed in the supernatural power of the Holy Spirit's communication to me, then I could have missed God's ultimate best for John and me. I cannot direct my own steps as it says in Jeremiah 10:23,

KEYS TO UNDERSTANDING

> O LORD, I know the way of man is not in himself; it is not in man who walks to direct his own steps (NKJV).

My life is rooted in Him as my faithful Savior to direct me in every area of my life. I am forever thankful that He is so faithful and good to me. As it says in Ephesians 1:17-19:

> I keep asking that the God of our Lord Jesus Christ, the glorious Father, may give you the Spirit of wisdom and revelation, so that you may know him better. I pray also that the eyes of your heart may be enlightened in order that you may know the hope to which he has called you, the riches of his glorious inheritance in the saints, and his incomparably great power for us who believe.

THREE

A Living Prophetic Word

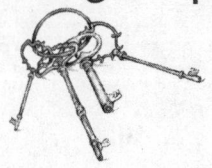

THE WAY A PROPHETIC WORD LIVES ON interests me intensely. Since it is direct communication from the Holy Spirit, it is as alive in the present as it was in the past and will be in the future. A revelatory word takes on and carries God's nature. It speaks as He speaks through the heavenly realm, which is a phenomenon, a process, we humans don't always understand or relate to. When the Holy Spirit gives us a revelation, it is just as true today as it was when the revelation was first received. For example, sometimes when you read a Bible verse that you've read a hundred times before, it suddenly takes in a whole new, deeper meaning than before. I'm not sure how it happens exactly, but when the Holy Spirit "touches" us, we are shown a fresh way of looking at things.

Caryl heard the Holy Spirit that evening in 1976, at just seventeen, with no idea of the journey she was beginning, no conscious thought that God was communicating to her and depositing something into her that would never die. She had no idea that a portion of it would unfold and come to birth twenty years later when we began a traveling ministry or that another portion would open thirty-two years later when we began leading mentoring groups at the International House of Prayer. The invitation and direct challenge from the Lord that she received and accepted in 1976 has had an ongoing energy in our lives. It was for then, it is also for now, and it will continue on into the future. We could not understand it fully at first, but now we know in our inner beings that He has challenged us to something great, something wonderful, something of Him. It is worth having faith and believing in what is not seen. Hebrews 11:1 says:

> **Now faith is the substance of things hoped for, the evidence of things not seen (NKJV).**

It is here we find Him . . . in a place of faith!

Often Caryl and I go back into our journals and check the things we recorded about the acts of God in our lives.

> **Then the LORD answered me and said: "Write the vision and make it plain on tablets, that he may run who reads it. For the vision is yet for an appointed time; but at the end it will speak, and it will not lie. Though it tarries, wait for it; because it will surely come, it will not tarry"** (Habakkuk 2:2-3, NKJV).

For many years we have gently encouraged people to write down their thoughts, prayers, and dreams, to write their words to God and to record every word from God. If we had not been encouraged to journal as young adults in our evangelical church, many of our answered prayers and God stories would only be distant memories or perhaps forgotten. Over the years, as we've recorded our conversations with God, we've built a library; we can go back to God's promises, look at them, and see God's faithfulness to us. What joy there must be in heaven for those who see the fulfillment of God's words on earth!

As a young girl, Caryl often heard her mother say, "God moves in mysterious ways." (William Cowper, "God Moves in a Mysterious Way," 1774) He does! We are constantly coming to understand more about God's actions in our past, in places where we didn't see what He was doing at the time. This continually speaks to us of His faithfulness and love in our lives.

It glorifies the Lord when it is His plan, His dream, His timing. It is a testimony to Jesus' work, a testimony to the faith that pleases the Father, when we can't quite grasp what He is setting up before us, but walk through in trust until He opens our eyes, and later we see.

These are the ways of God, designed for all His children to testify of Him. This is faith! Caryl and I believe there are many things about our lives and also about your lives that will utterly amaze us at the end. Many works of the Lord are still in the works, works He will and is fulfilling, things in action now that we will never see the fulfillment of until we reach Heaven and behold the Lord's beauty. All things we will understand in the end. That makes it totally worth living our lives in faith. It makes it A-OK to believe but not yet understand fully. We will understand it all on that day we reach Heaven.

Yes, Caryl and I can say that it is worth pushing through the obstacles that seem to rise up and stop us when we try to get closer to God and His plans. Sometimes we get bits and pieces of understanding about what He is doing; we witness the fulfillment of His purposes through our life history. God's not like us; He knows what He is saying and doing.

It is far more natural for us to live our lives according to what lines up in this world, isn't it? God's mindset is from a heavenly view; we look from an earthly perspective. Choosing to live in agreement with God's view, to live by faith and not by sight (2 Corinthians 5:7), has matured our faith. **It is maturity to believe and live according to what He says. Let's first line ourselves up with His Word and then believe and seek His supernatural expressions and activity in our lives.** This is why we seek the Holy Spirit and earnestly desire His spiritual gifts, especially prophecy (see 1 Corinthians 14).

FOUR

Change

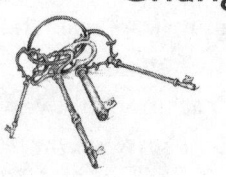

SEVERAL WEEKS after the celebration service at the Evanston Vineyard, we decided to visit another Vineyard church, one nearer our home. I figured that since something happened to me at a Vineyard church New Year's Eve service, perhaps someone at another Vineyard could tell me why my life was suddenly and dramatically different. Maybe they had the answer.

The closest Vineyard was in Elgin, Illinois. I wasn't sure where it was located, so I looked up their phone number to call for directions. The phone rang once, and a woman who answered said, "Hello, Vineyard Christian Fellowship of Elgin. How may I help you?" At first I thought it was an answering machine because it was late at night, and I was expecting to hear a prerecorded message giving me directions to the church. We talked for a few minutes. I told her we would be attending next Sunday with our friends the Neals. Then she gave me directions. When I hung up the phone, I was thrilled and so looking forward to Sunday. I wasn't sure how our children were going to adjust to a new church environment, but I was trusting that God was leading us to where He wanted us to be.

On Sunday morning, we drove over to the Neals' house and followed them down Randall Road to Elgin. I have never been as excited to get to church as I was that Sunday morning. I felt as if we were on our way to a divine appointment.

Walking into the lobby of the high school where the church met, I heard the worship team practicing—I still remember the song—*His Banner over Me Is Love*, from Song of Solomon 2:4. As practice continued, each song deeply moved me. They were expressive; many were similar to those I'd heard at the Evanston Vineyard several weeks before. They spoke of Gods' love for His people, piercing my heart again, this time with a greater impact. These songs were new to us.

As the music continued in the background, two women came up and warmly introduced themselves to us. They were the wives of the pastor and copastor and seemed to genuinely care that we were visiting. I felt loved by everyone I spoke to that Sunday. Upon entering the auditorium, it was quickly apparent that it was a small congregation, and everyone probably knew we were visitors. Initially, this made me feel slightly uncomfortable because at our former church visitors could attend services for months and still remain anonymous. There was no place to hide in this church! We found an empty row of seats and sat down. I remember a family sitting two rows in front of us turned around and introduced themselves. *These people are friendly*, I thought to myself. Their greetings were both sincere and refreshing. The service began and we enjoyed it. It took a few weeks of coming back, but we began to be drawn to the people and the pastor. We knew that God put this love into our hearts. We were welcomed and loved and we loved back. It was genuine love, and we knew it immediately.

When the meeting began, the tears came and I cried through every song. God's love was penetrating my heart and tenderizing it, touching me in deep ways that were new and unique to me. For the next several months, I cried through the worship songs every Sunday morning. God's love was flooding my mind and heart, and I could not contain it. At times our three children thought that something was wrong with Daddy. On more than one occasion, Caryl would lean over and whisper, "Are you OK, honey?" My only response was, "Could you give me another Kleenex, please?"

Though we did not always understand these encounters with God's love, each one always drew us closer to God. On a daily basis we prayed this simple prayer, "Lord, if this is from You, we want more, even though we don't understand what You are up to. If this is not from You, please take it away." We began by assuming God was somehow touching our lives in a way we had never imagined before. He always seemed very close to us during this season in our lives.

God was getting ready to redirect our plans in the blink of an eye. At first we were not aware of it. He had captured our hearts that New Year's Eve. I realize it is hard to defend the experiential. Experiences are subjective and usually cannot be quantified. Some people will dismiss our experiences as out-of-control emotionalism. They might even label us as "crazy charismatics." Out of the desire to tell our story in an honest and caring manner, we accept the risks of being written off. It's easy to dismiss what you don't understand. One of our life messages is that when we were first introduced to the ways of the Holy Spirit, we (and our friends the Neals) were evangelicals who had no one to talk to about what God was doing in our lives. It was a relief to finally meet a Vineyard pastor who helped me identify my prophetic gifting and point me in the right direction.

God is in the business of offending our minds to reveal our hearts. But God chose the foolish things of the world to shame the wise; God chose the weak things of the world to shame the strong (1 Corinthians 1:27). I make no apologies for what God has done in our lives. We have been fools for Christ on more than one occasion. All the misunderstandings we have gone through were worth it, as we grew deeper with God. Being misunderstood by men who don't know Him seems a small price to pay for more knowledge of the love of Christ. I urge you to be open to all the ways God wants to use you, and receive Him, welcome however He might want to communicate to you. He said,

> **Then you will call upon me and come and pray to me, and I will listen to you. You will seek me and find me when you seek me with all your heart** (Jeremiah 29:12-13).

Caryl and I both knew that despite our personal weakness, whatever God was stirring in our hearts was part of something much bigger than we were. More than our minds and souls were refreshed and awakened. We felt God was somehow drawing us closer to Him for a specific purpose, but how this fit into our normal and routine lives was uncertain to us. We knew He was giving us an invitation to follow Him.

FIVE

Our First Prophetic Conference

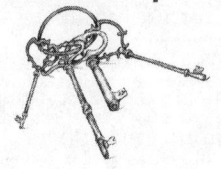

AT THE ELGIN VINEYARD we heard about Metro Vineyard Fellowship, a church in Kansas City, Missouri, with a rich prophetic history. It was founded on prophetic words, and in the early 1990s several prophetic men were on staff and in the congregation. Metro's pastor, Mike Bickle, had established a healthy place for prophetic people to worship and grow in their gifting.

Metro was linked with our new church home, the Elgin Vineyard Christian Fellowship. One Sunday morning it was announced that a family from Metro was going to be moving to Elgin specifically to start a prophetic nurture group at the Elgin Vineyard. That was great news! Trying to make this family feel welcomed, and out of my own curiosity, I asked our pastor if I could call down to Kansas City and talk to this guy who was going to lead the group. I had so many questions I wanted to ask him. I couldn't wait a few months until they moved to Elgin, so I began calling Bill Weinkauff on a regular basis. By the time they arrived in Elgin, we were finally introduced to Bill and Judy and their three children. They ended up renting a house in town that was near the church.

This nurture group was the same as a small group or home group that you would find in a typical church. We attended the prophetic nurture group under the leadership of Bill and Judy for four or five months. It was like giving a thirsty man a cup of cold water. This group was a real blessing to Caryl and me as we began to take baby steps in trying to hear God's voice. The Elgin prophetic nurture group was an offshoot of a larger Metro nurture group led by an older couple, Jim and Joyce Gochenour. The Gochenours were a wonderful mom and dad who helped many people to grow and develop in hearing God's voice. One weekend, Jim and Joyce came to visit the Elgin prophetic nurture group to model how to hear God's voice and to teach on healing. A couple who knew Jim and Joyce came with them and taught on healing. As a result of watching the Gochenours minister in our small group, our hunger grew even deeper for prophecy, healing, and prayer.

In the early '90s there was a lot of cross-pollination between Metro in Kansas City and the Elgin Vineyard. On one visit, Jim Goll came and taught on the prophetic. He modeled Christian maturity, taught, prayed, and left a deposit of the Spirit of God that continues to bear fruit. Caryl and I felt the reverberations of his influence at Elgin. In hearing about these men and women who were ahead of us in the ways of the Spirit, Caryl and I became eager to attend the next conference at Metro Christian Fellowship. We were excited to know there was a place to learn more about prophecy.

During the summer of 1993, we found ourselves on a plane headed for Kansas City. It was a special weekend for us because we were celebrating Caryl's thirty-fifth birthday and attending our first prophetic conference. As we stepped off the plane, the oppressive heat and humidity of the city hit us in the face. My first thought was, *How could anyone actually live here in this heat?* We proceeded to get a rental car and began the forty-five minute drive south to Grandview, Missouri, where the conference was located. About ten minutes after we left the airport, it began to rain on our car. At first I didn't think this was unusual because I thought it might be a "sun shower." I figured that since we had them in Illinois, Missouri must have them as well. I flicked on the windshield wipers just as a car drove by us in the other lane. It appeared dry and the windows were rolled down! Caryl and I both looked at each other without saying anything and then we looked up at the sky just to make sure a rain cloud wasn't directly overhead. There were no rain clouds anywhere. The sun was shining brightly and it was over one hundred degrees. About that time a truck drove past me in the left-hand lane; it was completely dry, too. After about one minute, the rain stopped as quickly as it had started. Just then we passed a sign near the road that said, "Welcome to Kansas City."

We both thought we were in a dream. *What on earth is going on?* I thought to myself. I remember asking Caryl, "It was raining on the car, right? And there were no rain clouds, right? Then why was it raining on just our car?" Like so many other events of the last six months, we could not explain it, but deep inside we knew God was drawing us closer to Himself. The problem was that we could not prove or convince anyone who wasn't there experiencing these things with us. We were on a journey, but didn't know where we were headed!

We arrived at Metro around lunchtime. The conference had begun and the morning session was over, but people were still lingering around the church. We sat in the bleachers at the back of the auditorium and began looking around. We noticed that people were sprawled out near the front of the church, lying on the carpet. What were they all doing lying on the carpet? I asked myself, *Am I in the right building?* Then Caryl and I began talking about television preachers we'd seen, the ones who would pray for people and then the people would fall over and drop to the floor. *Maybe that's what happened to them,* we thought. Our intentions were not to be negative or critical about what we saw, but we were trying to understand it, to make some sort of sense from it. Nothing in our church backgrounds came close to what we were seeing or experiencing. Our faith was childlike. I said to Caryl, "When we get back from lunch, let's go forward for prayer and see if we fall to the carpet like those people did." What did we have to lose? Since we were from out of state and didn't know anyone at the conference, we wanted to find out as much as we could in the short amount of time we were in Kansas City. If this church was phony, we wanted to find out sooner rather than later. We were determined not to be deceived; we only wanted genuine experiences with God!

After the afternoon teaching session, the main speaker called people forward for prayer or what they called "ministry time." Here was our chance, so I grasped Caryl's hand firmly as we headed to the front of the church. When we first got to the front, we noticed that most of the people who had come up for prayer had their eyes closed and their hands folded at their sides. I whispered to Caryl that we should do the same thing—so we wouldn't stand out from the rest. Not wanting to be deceived, I kept one eye open to see what was going on around me. I wasn't about to be tricked into anything. I didn't want some guy pushing me over as he prayed for me. I was smarter than that!

The speaker, who happened to be Jim Goll, began walking in front of people, laying his hands on their heads or shoulders. As this happened, most would start crying or fall backwards and be caught by someone who would gently assist them to the floor. It seemed genuine to me, but at the same time it was so foreign to my church experience. As the speaker approached us, my heart began to pound. I thought I was going to explode. As he came even closer, I whispered to Caryl to close her eyes because he would be in front of us in a few seconds. I remember closing my eyes and wondering what was going to happen next.

As Jim Goll walked in front of us he said, "There is a power ministry here." Within seconds we were both lying on the floor. My eyes were closed, and I was still holding on to Caryl's hand. What happened then may sound strange, but as I hit the floor, I immediately felt myself being lifted up at a high rate of speed. I sensed the same feeling in my stomach that comes when an elevator is going up. When the feeling of being lifted up stopped, I opened my eyes to find myself in a cloud at the gates of Heaven. I wasn't sure how I knew, but I knew it was Heaven. I had no concept of time, but I could still "see" with my eyes. My position was "face down," and I was lying on my stomach. At the time, I remember thinking how unusual this experience was, but on the other hand, I wasn't afraid. The first thing I immediately noticed were the flashes of different colored lights all around me. These flashes of light were different in color and intensity.

Just then I felt waves of love, affirmation, and acceptance coming out from Heaven and engulfing me. It felt so comforting. Even as I write and try to describe this feeling, no words really capture how I was feeling or what I was experiencing. Somehow, I sensed an invitation was being given to me to step over the threshold of Heaven and enter. My first reaction was to "say" no. In my heart, I felt that I was not worthy to take one step closer. In an instant, I was aware of all my own failures and shortcomings as a Christian. These thoughts wanted me to "run" away from this divine encounter. As more waves of love, affirmation, and acceptance kept washing over me, I was torn between feeling this invitation to come into the throne room and really knowing that my best was like filthy rags before God, and I was not worthy to enter Heaven and be in His presence. I was living Isaiah 64:6 that says, "All of us have become like one who is unclean, all our righteous acts are like filthy rags; we all shrivel up like a leaf, and like the wind our sins sweep us away." It's a bit hard to explain, but at some point I remember accepting this invitation and entering Heaven. I was face down several feet away from a throne. As I peered ahead, I could barely make out the steps leading up to this throne because they were engulfed in what appeared to be smoke or clouds. It was white in color. After this took place, a man riding a white horse came towards me and touched my shoulder with a sword. I immediately felt myself descending to earth—rather quickly, much the same way I had ascended.

Once I felt that I was "back in my body" I looked over at Caryl, who was still lying there next to me, and asked her, "Did you go anywhere?" She looked puzzled until I told her about my visit to Heaven. We were both shocked. *How could this be?* As we slowly got up off the floor, she said the Holy Spirit had touched her back. I said, "What do you mean?" As Caryl had lain on the floor, she felt God's presence as well as waves of electricity going up and down her back. It was a divine moment of feeling physically and spiritually touched by God. Caryl's back was her weak spot and had troubled her since childhood. Since this healing experience, Caryl has not had any back trouble. God touched Caryl's back in a supernatural way.

At the conference, we heard many speakers teach on revelation from God and on the benefits of hearing God's voice. On several occasions we received prayer from the ministry team. The worship was like none we had ever heard before. We felt God's presence and His affirmation throughout the whole conference. It was glorious. We left the conference wanting more of Jesus. Our spiritual gas tanks were filled to overflowing. Yet, at the same time, we had many unanswered questions. *Did I really go to Heaven? Was Caryl's back really healed? Was what we saw and heard about prophecy from the conference speakers biblical?* We left with more questions than we'd had before we came. After the conference, we were somewhat afraid to share any of our stories. We honestly thought no one would believe us and would think we were making things up to get attention.

We didn't know it at the time, but my trip to the gates of Heaven marked the beginning of a quest to understand and experience the words in Psalm 91,

He who dwells in the secret place of the Most High God shall abide under the shadow of the Almighty (NKJV).

More than once, God has taken initiatives to help me keep that goal alive. One strong encouragement came several years later while traveling and ministering in Austria with our friends Jim and Michal Ann Goll at a prophetic conference. Caryl had a dream about calling the Fire Department. In the dream, she picked up the phone and dialed 9-1-1. When she awoke we weren't sure exactly what the dream meant. At breakfast that morning, Jim asked if anyone had had any dreams they wanted to share. Caryl started sharing hers and we realized it was about Psalm 91:1. Some time after that, I read Bob Sorge's excellent book *Secrets of the Holy Place* about our secret place with God and how important it is to cultivate a secret life with God. Truly, answering God's call to live in Psalm 91:1, to dwell in the secret place of the Most High God and under His shadow, will be the only way to be safe from the 9-1-1's on earth, the natural, social, political, and economic changes, the emergencies of a planet combating global terrorism. Although it has been years since I was lifted from earth to the entry of the throne room, I am still journeying on to meet with God more fully in this secret place of intimacy.

In the months that followed the conference, we dove into the Scriptures and learned all we could about prophecy. There were more verses about prophecy, prophets, prophesying, and prophetesses than I ever remembered reading! I was amazed when I read the Old Testament's stories about the prophets again and again. Caryl and I wanted to learn more about prophecy and how to steward this gift. We wanted to understand it properly. **We believed that if God was going to give us specific spiritual gifts, it was our responsibility to learn, grow, and mature in whatever gifts He gave us.**

Children, in general, are natural students. They are teachable and sharp enough to discern the works of God for themselves. The Lord gave a gift to our children through this transition period by putting them into a church environment that was rich in the Holy Spirit. Although this spiritual atmosphere was a new culture for them, one they had never been exposed to, they instantly fell into the deeper waters of truth. Slowly, God was immersing us into a new church culture, one that we loved!

Our church family at the Elgin Vineyard was zealous to be touched personally by God. Our children found dear friends of their own age to share the world of loving Jesus that was opening up to all of us. It was a precious season, becoming like-minded with one another and our new friends. Although we were going through a difficult growth process of learning to listen to God and obey Him, through it all, we had tremendous support.

In our old environment, the focus had been on the written Word of God. God's Word is an absolutely essential and vital focus, but there is a hole, a void, if the Word is taught without the ministry of the Spirit. John 4:24 says that God is spirit, and his worshippers must worship in spirit and in truth. In the Vineyard we were introduced to new dimensions of the Holy Spirit breathing through God's Word. Our children grew, and the Lord laid foundations in them that He could build on the rest of their lives.

We learned that not only does the Holy Spirit love to minister to us personally, but also that through the Holy Spirit within us we can minister to the Lord. This was a new concept to us. We didn't know that we could minister to the Lord, let alone *how* we would go about doing this. Ezekiel 44:15 says:

> But the priests, who are Levites and descendants of Zadok and who faithfully carried out the duties of my sanctuary when the Israelites went astray from me, are to come near to minister before me . . . (*The Full Life Bible*, New International Version).

It amazed us to see that we can satisfy the Lord's heart through our worship and prayer to Him. This new dynamic was life-giving to us. It began to create a new world for our family as we found that the Lord Himself craves to be loved just as we long for Him to love us. Later this worship and prayer would be taken to a new level as we heard Mike Bickle's teaching on harp and bowl worship described in Revelation 5:8. We found ourselves soaking up this new revelation. It became a solid foundation, one that was cemented into us for the years to come.

First Timothy 4:14 also opened up a whole new dimension of prayer ministry for us. Paul said,

> **Do not neglect the gift that is in you, which was given to you by prophecy with the laying on of the hands of the eldership** (NKJV).

As the Holy Spirit breathed life on that principle, we began to pray more frequently with our children and friends—we prayed whenever we got the opportunity. The thrill of discovering new understandings of worship and prayer together wasn't all God had for us. It was also super exciting to see how He had set us into a perfect environment to cultivate our new and growing passionate hunger for Him.

Supernatural signs and spiritual impressions were all new to us. We were used to making our own plans and setting our own timetable. We were quickly reminded of several verses:

In his heart a man plans his course, but the LORD determines his steps (Proverbs 16:9).

A man's steps are directed by the Lord. How then can anyone understand his own way? (Proverbs 20:24).

We were slowly and steadily getting a first hand lesson in trusting God wherever He leads and in trusting that our steps would be determined by Him—and not by us! Proverbs 20:24 is really about giving God control over all aspects of your Christian walk. We knew this, but practically walking it out at times offended our minds.

SIX

More Change

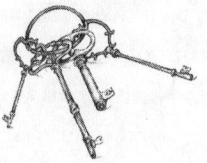

CARYL AND I SENSED THAT GOD might be giving us an invitation to move to Kansas City, but we weren't exactly sure what this was going to look like. The idea seemed absurd. We both had been born and raised in Illinois and all our friends and family lived near us. The notion of moving had never crossed our minds, until now. We desperately wanted to live in a place where our whole family could flourish spiritually, regardless of the cost involved.

So as we considered a move to Kansas City, it seemed to us like only one of several options. Another option was to stay in the area so I could finish the graduate degree I had recently begun. At the time I was taking one evening class a semester and working my regular sales job during the day. If I quit my job and we downsized, I could attend school full time and graduate in one year with a degree in clinical psychology. This would allow me a fresh start in a new career. At this point, all the options seemed reasonable, but we wanted God's best for our family.

If we did end up moving, it would definitely encourage us to grow spiritually and Metro would be a great place to "plant" our children. We loved our little house in Crystal Lake, but we wanted to go deeper in all that God had for us. We wanted to be radically obedient. We wanted whatever God wanted, regardless of what that looked like.

One evening after we put our children to bed, we sat in the living room to pray about our future. It was the fall of 1993, and we were crying out to God for direction. We felt as if we had to do something. I vividly remember praying, "God, I am putting my job on the altar. Do with it whatever You please. If You want us to move to Kansas City, You have to show us clearly. God, You are the desire of our hearts; if You have a better plan for us and our children, please show us." This was a difficult prayer to pray because I was enjoying my job—I sold industrial metals in a five-state territory. It also meant breaking family ties and friendships because Caryl's father was the regional manager of our office and had brought me into the work some eleven years earlier.

That simple prayer was to be a huge turning point in our journey. I immediately had a vision of two silos, the kind that are several stories high used for grain storage on farms. I somehow knew that one silo represented our finances, and the other silo represented friends. I sensed the Lord saying, "I am going to drain the financial silo, but your other silo will be full." At the time, I had not fully grasped what God was saying to us.

Several days later, I had a vision of God's hand turning off a water sprinkler; somehow I knew that it had to do with our finances. At least God was telling us ahead of time what He was about to do! In His goodness, He was preparing our hearts to walk in faith. Another night while praying by myself, I had an odd experience. I was sitting on my couch with my eyes closed. Immediately I felt a sensation I can only describe as feeling like being turned upside down. I quickly opened my eyes, but I was still sitting upright on the couch. Once again I closed my eyes and bowed my head to pray, and again the same sensation occurred; only this time, as I felt myself being turned upside down, I literally heard coins dropping out of my pockets and hitting the floor. There are so many times in our lives when God is speaking something, and it takes a while to have the full understanding of what He's saying to us at the time.

Sure enough, within days of this experience I started losing major accounts at work. Without explanation and rather suddenly, accounts that had been loyal customers for years and years began buying from our competitors. After several months of losing major accounts, my income took a sharp dive. I was in a financial trial.

As the weeks went by, my sales were decreasing faster than anyone could imagine. This was highly unusual because our industry remained stable and never experienced extreme fluctuations. On top of that, I was the only salesman in our office experiencing this huge decline in sales. At this point Caryl's father had retired, and I had a new boss. I was called into his office one day, and he asked me what was happening. I shook my head and simply said, "I don't know." He knew that the sudden decrease in sales would directly affect my monthly commission checks. I remember him saying, "You'll never recover from this."

Several weeks after talking with my boss, I burst into tears as I drove into our driveway after a particularly difficult day at work. Caryl met me outside. I told her about yet another major account I had lost and how everything at work seemed to be going wrong. She gently reminded me by saying, "Remember when you prayed about your job? You told God to take it away if He wanted. I think that's exactly what He's doing." Slowly we began finding some sort of comfort in knowing that maybe God was really behind this, and He was redirecting our path. This was definitely *not* the way we were used to God leading us. However frustration turned into excitement, and before long I was rejoicing that I was losing accounts. Imagine that! We never thought that God would get our attention this way, but it was obvious to everyone around us that God was definitely up to something with our family.

When a friend offered to rent us her home while she attended a downstate university, it made perfect sense to us to begin our journey by putting our home on the market so we could stay in town and I could finish my graduate degree. We thought for sure that we would stay in Illinois; I would quit my job to finish graduate school. Then we would eventually move to Kansas City.

On the practical side of our decision-making process, staying in Illinois seemed like a great idea. On the impractical side, it looked as if God was inviting us to walk by faith and be obedient to follow where He was leading. We wanted both sides. At this point, our faith was the size of a mustard seed. Our plan was that we did not have a clear plan. Our children trusted; they were not upset because they were walking with us on our faith journey. Our family continued to attend the Elgin Vineyard, where we were growing in our faith and understanding of what our future might hold for us.

SEVEN

Moving On

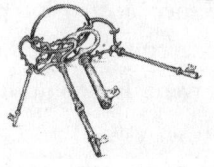

DURING THE NEXT FEW MONTHS, we did a lot of trying to explain things we didn't quite understand. Caryl and I felt like teenagers again. We had great eagerness to venture off to follow Jesus without adequate reasoning. Even though it felt as if we didn't have all the pieces to the puzzle, we continued to walk ahead, trusting in God to direct us to exactly where He wanted us. Our faith was childlike.

Our great loving extended family could not track with us. They wanted to support us, but trying to make sense of our vague, abstract plans was very difficult. It did not make sense because they did not understand our new prophetic gifts. It was difficult to explain because it was so new to us; we weren't sure *how* to explain it. My in-laws have always lavishly poured out their love and support into our lives and especially into the lives of their grandchildren. They wanted the best for us. It was a faith journey for them, too. It was a sweet time, but a very tense time as well.

I wasn't sure if it was stupidity or walking by faith, but we decided to "walk it out." So the week of Thanksgiving we listed our house with a local realtor. She suggested that we wait until after the holidays because December was a terrible month to sell houses, but we went ahead and put it on the market anyway. Real estate sales were slow back then because new homes in the area were priced lower than older ones. Our home was a small older home on an historical street. It was so lovely with mature trees. We had often been told that it was one of the most popular streets in the town, so we anticipated a quick sale. But no calls came in December. We were beginning to wonder if our house would sell at all.

We thought that after we took one step in faith, it would be God's "turn" to take the next step for us. Once again, God proved Himself to be faithful. Around this time, God was starting to teach me about obedience and trust, no matter what the costs were. He could have done this in any number of ways, but the way He chose was a bit of a surprise to me. He began to highlight certain days of every month that would hold keys to help us understand our future. These "keys" would open doors that we were to walk through as a family so that wisdom and revelation about our future would be given to us. I named these days, "Door Days." Every month, for the next twelve months, the Holy Spirit gave me days that He assigned as "Door Days" to mark on my calendar. We would pray about those days with great anticipation. It was fun and exciting for us as we gathered our children to pray and wait.

We really looked forward to Door Days. They were significant because the revelations were like bread crumbs leading us down to Metro. They confirmed a lot of what we were praying about. Sometimes the revelation came in dreams; sometimes thoughts came to us, and we prayed about them. What He gave us always was applicable to what we were experiencing at the time. This fresh revelation was like giving a thirsty man a drink of water. We needed it; it helped sustain us and increased our wavering faith. These Door Days weren't something that we shared with just anybody. We knew our experience was a bit on "the edge" but God always met us powerfully on those dates.

We received a call from our realtor in mid-February; she wanted to show the house in an hour. I got off the phone and we quickly started to clean up and put the toys away. While I was vacuuming, I sensed the Lord saying, "This will be the last time you'll vacuum this house." I was a bit puzzled and really didn't know what He meant. Several minutes later I had an impression from the Lord that we were to take the first offer from any prospective buyers. I tried to convince myself that this impression was *not* from God, but as the evening went on, I knew I had to be obedient to what God was asking me to do. During the showing while we waited at our friend's house, the realtor called and told me the people who had looked at the house were going to place an offer that evening. After we returned home, we received another call from the realtor with the offer.

On hearing the amount and terms of the contract I said, "I'll agree to those terms." Over the next several days we finalized the contract and found ourselves needing to move out in sixty days. The great news was that we had sold the house. The bad news was that we had no clue where we were moving to!! It was exciting and dreadful at the same time. It seemed that God was not in any big hurry to tell us what to do next.

Since renting from our friend had fallen through, our immediate plan was to move in with Caryl's parents. At this point we weren't sure if we would be moving to Kansas City or buying another house in the area. It was a bit confusing to us as well as to family members who were watching us and waiting to see where we would finally end up! On moving day we needed to put the majority of our belongings into a storage facility. With all this dismantling, we all felt very tender and especially vulnerable.

Beginning to doubt ourselves and our ability to make rational decisions, we asked God to confirm our possible move to Kansas City on the next Door Day with signs and wonders. We really needed God to confirm what our next step might be in a dramatic fashion. He did not disappoint. This is what happened on the next Door Day.

That morning as I was driving to work, the expressway traffic was unusually backed up. It was a cloudy, overcast winter day and it had just begun to drizzle and sleet at the same time. Most of the cars on the road were dirty. A semi-trailer was in front of me, and I felt a strong impression to go into the other lane and pass the truck. I actually thought that God wanted to show me something.

KEYS TO UNDERSTANDING

At first I resisted because I wasn't sure where this impression or sense had come from. It was pretty early in the morning and usually my commute to work was uneventful. The longer I resisted, the stronger the impression became. I finally gave in and changed lanes to pass the slow-moving semi. Much to my surprise, I saw another semi-trailer directly in front of the truck I'd just passed. It was pure white, spotless, with shining bumpers, and looked as if it had just been washed. As I passed by, huge black block letters on the trailer that read, Kansas City, Missouri, jumped out at me from the pure white truck. It was surreal. That was the first and last time I've ever seen a truck with the name of a city and state emblazoned across its side in such huge letters. There was no other writing on the truck or on the cab. The whole truck had a dream-like quality about it—immaculately white, with bright chrome bumpers, in Chicago morning rush hour traffic on a slushy morning. I almost drove off the road. In a semi-panic, I called Caryl on the cell phone to tell her every detail. Wow! That was pretty dramatic, but we continued to pray for more signs to confirm this "Kansas City" sign—one just wasn't enough.

Another "promise" that God gave Caryl during this time was that He would confirm our decision to move by sending us out with the wind of His Spirit. Those were very comforting and reassuring words, but we did not know exactly how the "wind" would figure into our moving. Later, when we moved, it would be revealed in a rather dramatic fashion.

Seeking additional and desperately needed direction, I decided to call some people in Kansas City. I began "searching out the land" by making phone calls to people who had moved to Kansas City and were attending Metro. This bridge of people began with the Weinkauffs, who had come up to our Chicagoland church from the Gochenour nurture group in Kansas City. God had formed a community of Metro people for the Weinkauffs and Gochenours that we naturally fell right into step with. My calls consisted of asking one question, "How did you know God was calling you to Kansas City?" A similar thread telling of the Lord's invitation ran through many of their stories. Their input was priceless, and later we would become friends with everyone I had called.

Slowly, through these introductory phone calls, we began to get to know some of the families in the subdivision. Each couple told us their stories of how God had moved them to Kansas City to be part of Metro under the leadership of Mike and Diane Bickle. Each story had a different flavor, but the same themes ran through all—wanting to be part of a prophetic Christian community, attend Metro, and a sense of God's invitation to be there.

Caryl and I had always believed that God gives us invitations to partner with Him. We had a growing feeling that this is what He was doing in us. For whatever reason, He was inviting us to partner with Him in serving the church with the spirit of revelation described in Ephesians 1:17. In our hearts, we wanted to obey and agree with what He was speaking to us. After we took the first major step and sold our house in Crystal Lake, the Lord started to open the doors one by one, slowly leading us to Kansas City. There we found out the importance of what we were saying yes to.

Caryl and I prayed and decided to take another step of faith. We reasoned that if we did move to Kansas City, we wanted to live and raise our children in a community that reflected Ephesians 1:17-18 believers:

> **I keep asking that the God of our Lord Jesus Christ, the glorious Father, may give you the Spirit of wisdom and revelation, so that you may know him better. I pray also that the eyes of your heart may be enlightened in order that you may know the hope to which he has called you, the riches of his glorious inheritance in the saints.**

In Kansas City there was a Holy Spirit community of believers who were going after God's heart and trying to hear His voice in faith. It was a place where God seemed to speak often. We wanted to learn how to hear God's voice, too, as a family. This sounded too good to be true. It's as if we were stepping into Acts 2: 42-47.

So in late February, Caryl and I continued our journey by taking a fact-finding trip to Kansas City. It was our desire to visit and personally meet the people we'd talked with on the phone that were in the Metro community. At this point, we really were not looking for a home to buy but trying to deepen our understanding of whether or not this was where God wanted us. To do this successfully, we wanted to see Metro outside the lens of a conference setting. God did not disappoint us on this trip.

Early on, I'd decided to keep up with a man named Kirk Bennett. I spoke to him several times after meeting him at our first conference. Kirk was prophetically gifted, and his family was established at Metro. Over the phone, I reconnected with Kirk and told him we were coming for another visit. Kirk and Dee Bennett invited us to visit their home group when we came to town. They also mentioned that a group from their neighborhood was going to meet for dinner, and they invited us to join them and personally meet people from the church community who might become our friends and neighbors someday.

Caryl and I were eager to reconnect with Jim and Joyce Gochenour as well. I called Jim on the phone, and he said we could visit their prophetic group, which fortunately met the weekend we would to be in town. Sunday we planned on attending church at Metro, so our weekend was filled up before we arrived. We were thrilled. Every day, through each person we met, God revealed a new aspect of His faithfulness. We had a chance to get to know Jim and Joyce a little better and thought that our connection with them would be important. We wanted to be mentored by them and could see ourselves becoming part of their prophetic group.

Bennetts' home group prayed for us, and we soaked up every drop they poured out on us. They lived in an area with prophetic history. As we drove through their neighborhood for the first time, the day was wintry and overcast. We tried to imagine ourselves living there. It was difficult at first because Caryl is an artist and has always been visually sensitive. This place did not inspire her or satisfy her visually. "This place could use a lot more flowers," Caryl thought to herself. Only later did we realize how important this trip would turn out to be.

Sunday at church was fantastic. The worship was uplifting, and the message was encouraging. After the service, the Bennetts introduced us to several more families from their neighborhood that attended Metro. We were briefly introduced to Mike and Diane Bickle, one of many families who lived in the subdivision where the Bennetts lived. Mike was warm and outgoing and welcomed us. As we left the service and walked to our rental car, we began talking.

God was tugging on our hearts, calling us to engage in a commitment that later would bring us into a lifestyle that depended on hearing His voice and following Him. We sensed this was a departure from our normal understanding of Christianity. This seemed radical. We thought, *What is this invitation He is giving us that's is pulling on our hearts and drawing us closer to Him?* Before we went back to the airport, we agreed to take one more ride through the Bennetts' neighborhood to drive by a few houses that we had seen for sale a few days earlier.

This was our starting point because many transplanted families who had moved to Kansas City to attend Metro lived in this small, prophetic community. It was an old military base with duplexes that had been sold to the general public. I estimate about thirty families lived there, many with children like ours, attended Metro. After a quick drive through the neighborhood, we headed back to the airport to catch our plane back to Chicago.

When we got home to Illinois, we continued to dialogue with each other and pray. We had so much to share with our children; by now we were starting to actually envision ourselves in Kansas City. Since we already had a signed contract on our house, we were definitely looking ahead for additional housing options.

EIGHT

Wind of the Spirit

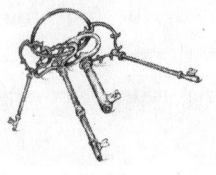

APRIL THE 14, 1994, the day before we moved, was also our last day to receive mail. We had been anxiously awaiting news from Kansas University to see if I had been accepted into their graduate program in clinical psychology. That morning the postman left the letter notifying me that I was not accepted into their graduate program. It seemed odd, as my grade point average was an A minus. This was news we did not want to hear, and it hit us like a ton of bricks. There went our practical plan!

Here we were, beginning to move out of the house we had been raising our children in, confidently thinking that attending graduate school would "get us" to Kansas City. When that door shut, we did not have a clue about what God was up to. On finding out that my application was denied, all we could see ahead of us was moving into my in-laws' basement for who knows how long! Our situation seemed hopeless, and we thought our lives were going to crash.

We didn't tell the children right away because they were a bit too young to fully comprehend the emotional turmoil we were going through. Caryl and I went to bed that evening drained physically drained and questioning God. Had we missed it? Had it been wrong to sell our house without a place to move to? Could we ever recover from this huge mistake, if it had been a mistake at all?

Our moving day just happened to fall on April 15, tax deadline day. The morning started with extremely windy weather. We were so emotionally frayed that we had forgotten about the promise of being sent out by the "wind of the Spirit." Sometime during the morning, Caryl remembered God's promise to her and shared it with me. It seemed like a holy moment. Could God really be in this move? Was it only a coincidence that today was a day with extremely high winds?

That day Caryl and I wanted to create a memory for our children, one they could look back on, hopefully with fond recollections of moving out of their house. Over the years, we often marked important events in our lives and the lives of the children by celebrating them, so we decided to take the children to our family's favorite restaurant. Since breakfasts at the Colonial had been a family tradition, before we officially moved, we went there one last time.

Caryl and I were extremely emotional. The events of the past few months had finally caught up with us. We had just given up our secure life for an unknown future. Tears were running down our faces as the waitress came to take our order. Since I am the comedian in our family, I informed her that we were not experiencing a death, just a move to an unknown city. This was the beginning of our crazy ride of looking like fools for Christ.

The process of change and transformation continued on many levels. After we closed on the house, the kids wanted to go back one last time to say good-bye to their bedrooms and retrieve a toy from the back yard. On arriving at our old home, Caryl began weeping intensely. The house was empty to Caryl. The Lord led Caryl through this loss by asking her to yield to the Holy Spirit all that was in her heart for her home—all her natural instincts—the need, love, and desire for a home that God puts in women's hearts. The Holy Spirit had worked in Caryl to create a loving home within the walls of our little house. Now, not only was the house gone, she sensed that He had left it too. That was a strong feeling to experience.

Our minds were filled with all the memories of raising our children in that nice little home. **We came face to face with what it meant to take up our crosses and follow Him. Saying yes to Jesus involved more denying ourselves than I ever imagined.** We were beginning to understand the costs involved in laying our lives down. We couldn't see then how the Holy Spirit was teaching us and preparing us—all of us—to begin to let go and step into a lifestyle of prayer and fasting—an important part of our history with God and part of our current call to prayer.

As devastating as the news about KU was, it was just an emotional shock; it did not destroy our faith or the momentum moving us toward Kansas City. We continually talked together about the possibility that God might be moving us there. We discussed all the implications of moving— the obvious ones, of course, were leaving our family and friends. We all agreed that we wanted to be led by God as a family and that we would follow Him. Everyone's vote counted! We agreed to pray together as a family to seek God's will for all of us.

Over the next six weeks, God began to confirm the stirrings in our hearts and in the hearts of our children that a move to Kansas City could be possible. These stories took our faith to a new level. God seemed so close to us during this time.

NINE

Our New Duplex

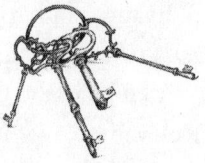

THAT SUMMER, we decided that it was essential to take the children to the 1994 *Passion for Jesus* conference at Metro. We had been including them in our discussions about the looming possibility of moving, but they were also getting excited about it on their own. One of LeAnn and Erin's friends, Amy, was moving back to Kansas. This dear little friend was the daughter of Bill and Judy Weinkauff. Their work was done, and God was moving them back to Kansas City to rejoin the Gochenours' group. The timing was priceless—we saw ourselves as two families venturing out to follow God. We were being led to Kansas City simultaneously, no matter what it cost us.

All three girls were talking and praying about going to Kansas City as they joined arm in arm, elbow to elbow. They prayed and then would wait on Jesus together—knowing that in faith their prayers would be answered. They were ahead of us and wanted to go on this journey together; they prayed for the release for both of our families. They were ready to leave our familiar life for a new one if God was exciting and real, and Amy was coming too. And God did show himself to be very real to these girls in ways that Caryl and I couldn't fathom. Seeing how He brought them closer to Himself and each other strengthened all of us adults.

Watching the girls from the sidelines brought our seven-year-old, John Brendan, and the Weinkauffs' two sons right into agreement. Will, four years older, and David, four years younger, were like brothers to Brendan. They caught something from the girls, and their hearts burned too; it was as addicting as laughter. Brendan knew that if we moved, he would have instant friends nearby.

All our children were dreaming dreams, and to this day we firmly believe that God was preparing them. LeAnn and Erin both dreamt that God was making a new place ready for our family. Can you imagine the sweet enthusiasm of a nine- and an eleven-year-old telling me this over their bowls of breakfast cereal as little seven-year-old John Brendan chimed in agreement to all his sisters believed in? It was amazing. Not only were Caryl and I excited about our children preparing to move, but we were also amazed and encouraged by the timing. It didn't feel like an accident that the family who had led the prophetic nurture group in Elgin was also moving back to Kansas City.

The girls weren't the only ones to receive dreams and visions. About a week before we left for Kansas City, I had a dream. The Lord clearly gave me two numbers 711 and 713. At the time I wasn't able to tell if these numbers were moving dates or house numbers. I wasn't sure what the street name was. Toward the end of the dream, I walked into the living room of a home and, proceeded out the back door, and looked across the back yard. As I was looking at the neighbor's house, I noticed a rabbit in a wire cage. I woke up from the dream not really understanding all the details. I prayed for understanding because this dream just seemed a bit odd to me. This was the first time I'd had a rabbit in one of my dreams.

Then the day before we left for the conference, the Lord gave Caryl a dream. She saw the Lord in our kitchen preparing a meal for us. He had white hair and a long white beard. The Lord himself assisted us to our car with our suitcases. This really spoke to us. We were encouraged to believe that He was taking care of every detail for us. He is full of wisdom and all knowing; we could fully trust Him for the next big step of faith.

At that time, our oldest daughter, LeAnn, desired a fruitful place where she could create a garden of her very own. I assured her I would take this into consideration! Later, we found out that God had heard her prayer and taken it literally and seriously.

The conference of 1994 was another great learning experience for us. Not only did we enjoy the conference, but we also reconnected with many of the people we had met in February. As soon as the conference was over, we set our sights on purchasing a home, hopefully in the Bennetts' neighborhood. We were making a choice to live in a community of believers from Metro. The appearance of the neighborhood, with its military homes, was not appealing to us. This was another place where we had to yield our flesh to the Lord because this area would not have been our first choice. We all agreed that if we were going to move, we wanted to be in a neighborhood where the Bennetts lived. At this point, we had heard so many encouraging stories about the area.

As we approached the first house for sale in the neighborhood, we immediately saw that the entire front of the house was brightened by a variety of colorful flowers. We later found out that the duplex owner was a horticulturist. *This is too good to be true* we thought. Could this be the Lord's heart? To flood us with color in this neighborhood? Could it be the Lord's heart to show that He cares for a child's desire for a garden? We called the realtor, and she said she would drive over to show us the home.

Upon entering the duplex, for some reason I immediately walked through the living room, through the kitchen, and into the backyard. Caryl stayed in the front room and talked with the realtor. I looked at the neighbor's house and saw a rabbit in a wire cage exactly like the one in my dream. I walked back inside and asked the realtor, "What's the address of this home?" She responded, "713." I then asked, "What is the neighbor's address?" She responded, "711." I looked at Caryl and said, "This is the house from my dream. This is our house, selected by God specifically for our family." The realtor looked at us as if to say, "Yeah, right buddy."

The realtor said two other bids had already been submitted on this particular home and our chance of getting it was almost zero. What the realtor didn't know was God had already begun to work for us behind the scenes.

The day we spotted the house, even before we made our appointment to view it with the realtor, we had met the next door neighbor, Kellie. The Fenimores, a Metro family, lived in the 711 duplex. That morning Kellie had been watering her flowers with her four-year-old son Josh. Kellie became our instant friend. She put in a good word for us that afternoon to the owners of 713. I insisted the realtor present our bid to the homeowners. We then rushed back to the airport and flew back to Chicago. Two days later we received a call from the realtor; she told us that we were the proud owners of the duplex at 713. Yea, God! He loves us so much that He even picked out the right house for us.

Another kiss from God was the horse pasture that backed up to our little backyard. Our girls had taken riding lessons in Illinois and had had to give that up when we moved. At night, we walked to the back of our yard and fed the horses through the chain-link fence.

At first, I was not sure why the Lord highlighted the number 711 in my dream. Our soon-to-be neighbors at 711 were Brian and Kellie Fenimore and their three wonderful children. The Fenimores ended up being our neighbors for over eleven years, and we remain good friends to this day. Brian and Kellie have an itinerant ministry teaching on the Father's Heart of God, and they move in the gifts of prophecy and healing. Often we had meals together, talked about spiritual things for hours at our fence, or just hung out together with our kids as they jumped on our trampoline. The Fenimores are a real blessing to us. Our children grew up being like cousins to each other. We met Jim and Michal Ann Goll through the Fenimores. Brian worked for the Goll's ministry. It was in this setting that we became friends with Jim and Michal Ann, sharing life together by watching each other's kids or playing and talking in our backyards.

As part of this spiritual community, it was especially nice to have Mike and Diane Bickle living near us as neighbors. We would say hi to Diane often when she picked up their mail. The mailboxes for our particular street were located right in front of our house. In His grace, God surrounded us with godly models to follow and brought people into our lives to help nurture the gifts He'd placed in us. We look back with fond memories to our early days in Kansas City.

We've wondered, *were Caryl's thoughts a prayer that went right up into Heaven, its answer already given, hidden in the multitude of flowers that lay dormant in the February gloom over our future home?* If so, God was answering both Caryl's prayer and LeAnn's desire. Now, as we look back, we realize that LeAnn's prayer was very prophetic. She longed for a garden. Our move to Kansas City would unlock for her future a garden enclosed, as in Song of Solomon 4:12,15-16. Not only did the Lord have flowers bursting out in our little neck of the neighborhood, but He also had rich, spiritual gardens planned for our children's destiny, for their future.

Our little LeAnn at this time had a burning desire for worship, piano, and voice. She was one of the oldest of the many children we instantly befriended in our neighborhood. Many of the families homeschooled. Our daughters almost instantly began leading the way for other children with similar interests. When LeAnn was only fourteen and Erin was just twelve, they began teaching piano lessons to neighborhood children as part of a homeschool venture.

Caryl had a clear dream of LeAnn shortly after our arrival in Kansas. LeAnn was leading a row of children through a beautiful scene of mountains, lakes, and valleys. She plowed the way as a natural leader. Although there were no literal lakes, mountains, or valleys in this military subdivision, we sensed the great beauty of Heaven's mountains, valleys, and lakes—the "gardens of eternity" we cultivate when we live in God's will. And we are so blessed to work in such a place of beauty!

TEN

A New Season

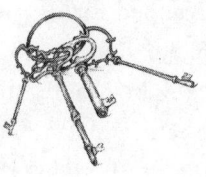

A NEW PHASE OF OUR JOURNEY BEGAN when we left friends, family, and my job to move to Kansas City—for us another step into the unknown. It felt really strange. Some people important to us opposed our move, and we started to doubt ourselves. Whoever heard of a guy leaving a great sales job with a great company, great benefits, a weekly paycheck, and a bright future to move to a strange city with no friends, no job, and no support? Did I mention that I was the first salesman to quit in the company's ninety-five-year history? I can vividly remember that last day at work. I had said my good-byes; I walked out the building and across the parking lot toward my car. I opened the car door to get in, put the keys into the ignition, and stared out the window. The first thing I did was take off my tie, and as soon as I did this I sensed the Lord saying, "You'll be working for Me now. You'll be working for Me full-time." Deep within our souls, Caryl and I knew it was the right move to make. It was the only move. We moved to Kansas City out of obedience to the One who had called us. The pain we felt as we left friends and family behind on August 28, 1994, was beyond words.

Prayer was a big part of our family's desire to make a memory. We truly wanted the day to be significant to our family for generations to come! When we all prayed, Caryl felt that the Lord gave her August 28, 1994. This represented Romans 8:28, our family life verse,

> **And we know that in all things God works for the good of those who love him, who have been called according to his purpose.**

Over the years we have reminded God of His promise to our family. (August is the eighth month of the year . . . hence 8:28).

We had no idea what God had planned for us. Now it's clear that He wanted to train and equip us in prophetic ministry so that we could go out to encourage and comfort others. He also wanted to train us to mentor people who were budding in prophetic gifts or beginning to move in prophetic ministries. The problem is that He didn't tell us that right away. It took several years to see His plan. Did we feel unprepared and weak in the knees? You bet! We never went to seminary. I have a Bachelor of Science degree in sociology and Caryl has an art degree. No one ever sat us down and explained to us how to do ministry, let alone prophetic ministry. We were enrolled in the School of Hard Knocks. That's a tough way to earn a degree!

We spent several of our early years in Kansas City trying to deny our prophetic calling and wiggle our way away from it. Initially, I continued to be embarrassed to talk about my newfound gift. It was awkward for me to admit to someone that I hear from God.

In many ways I felt caught between worlds—the familiar world I grew up in and the new world where God reigns and wants to use us. Caryl and I often said to each other, "This is not what we signed up for." Though God stretched us in many ways, we could not go back to our old ways of Christian living with a business-as-usual approach to life.

Over the years, I have received all kinds of strange looks when people find that out that I hear from God. I have learned to "fly under the radar" because I found out quickly that some people are hostile toward prophetic people. My gifting is definitely not something I wear as a badge. Once, on learning that I had a traveling ministry, a family member said to me, "Why would anyone want to listen to you?" Not exactly the response I was hoping to hear!

However, sometime during 1998 after we'd been ordained and had officially registered Praiseworthy Ministry with the state, I realized that my heart had changed. I saw that God was setting up divine appointments with people He wanted to minister to through me. I concluded that it was time for me to step up to the plate and begin acting according to the way God created me. **Humility wasn't hiding and running from my calling. Humility was agreeing with God and growing in my gifting.** I no longer tried to hide from what God was calling me to be and do. I don't remember a specific day, but somewhere, somehow, I had grown up.

About that time in '98 Jim Goll made our ministry an affiliate of his organization, and friends and mentors independently confirmed that God wanted me to be an itinerant prophetic minister. Gradually I was becoming comfortable in who I was and in how God had gifted me. I was by no means an expert on prophecy, but I did gain experience. By Janaury 2009, I either personally lead or directly participated in over two hundred conferences and meetings.

While ten years of involvement in prophetic ministry may strike the reader as a bit of experience, I do not view it that way. I still felt inadequate and inexperienced when people invited me to minister. I've often wondered God won't lift this calling from me and give it to someone more qualified.

It always helps to look back in my journals and read over all the prophetic words we've received affirming our gifting and calling. The first time I did this, back in '98, I was amazed! I had forgotten about many of them. Dust collects over these promises, and I need to read them again and again. Even as I write these pages, I have returned to my journals and reread them all again, several times each, from 1993 to the present.

Let me encourage you to keep a journal. When doubts or fears invade your mind about your destiny in God, you can read the truth about what God says about you. I am surprised at how often I review the prophetic promises we have received over the years. Here are just a few examples from my journal:

SUMMER 1993. PASSION FOR JESUS CONFERENCE. God has given you a power ministry. There's going to be angelic activity. Fifteen thousand volts of electricity.

OCTOBER 15, 1995. METRO CHRISTIAN FELLOWSHIP. I see the Spirit of the Lord resting on you mightily, John and Caryl. In the name of Jesus, we thank you for sending them here from Chicago and planting them in this house of the Lord. They're growing up. I see saplings. They're growing from tender shoots into saplings in prophetic ministry. We bless that ministry, Lord, that you have given them and entrusted to them. We pray, Father, that you would use them powerfully in leadership and impartation and mentoring also in the days ahead in this house. They will be fruitful. I see them as fruitful trees. Young ones [will be] growing up underneath them, like an orchard, as the years go on.

OCTOBER 15, 1995. METRO CHRISTIAN FELLOWSHIP. I want to go back to the O'Shaughnessys. . . . You are at the right place at the right time and do not listen to that word that got assigned against you from authority saying you missed the mark, you blew it; you lost your job for no good reason. And I cancel that word of accusation that was released against you, and I speak hope back into the loins of your mind, and I say you've come; you're being tutored; you're not lost in the crowd. God knows your name. He knows your address. He knows your birthright and that you've come here at the right place and the right time to receive an impartation even this night to be a dreamer in the House of the Lord. I even speak forth a

Joseph-type anointing to be upon you, to be a dreamer ahead of time and to receive this impartation of a dreamer—even of economic understanding in Jesus' name.

JULY 7, 1997. AUSTRIA. In Isaiah 30 it says in quietness and in confidence shall be your strength. And the Lord has been taking you into this season of quietness and you have felt like an ugly duckling. You've known that something new is hatching forth in your life, but you've been in the season of change. Who am I anyway? What was I born for? What am I doing? And you will continue in a season of change, but you are just now beginning to find out who you are, what you were born for, and what you will be doing. You just put on your new shoes, shoes of prophetic teachers, and you will wear these shoes with confidence and security, and the Lord will come to you in this next season, and He will be your teacher, and you will quietly wait on the Lord. You will have more time free than you have time of work, and this is the Lord. You will have the time for the Lord to be your teacher, where the Scriptures will be your friend in a new way. And this woman (Caryl) shall blossom forth with the perfume of the prophetic as a restorer of the prophetic arts. She will teach people that they were created to release the aroma of God's fragrance. And you will do seminars, and you will do gatherings, and you will do small groups on teaching people how to paint, and there will be a poetic stream that will come forth from out of you. You will begin to prophesy in poetry, and there is a writing gift that will come forth. So wear your shoes of prophetic teachers with grace and humility, and you will be greatly surprised at the people who your lives will impact. Amen.

ELEVEN

Prophetic Training: In the School of Humility

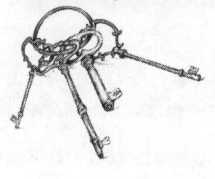

IT SEEMED ODD TO ME that God was calling us to move to Kansas City before He mentioned anything about the employment He had waiting for me. At first, I was sure He would line up a job for me before we moved but that did not happen. I contacted four employment agencies in Missouri six months before we moved and faxed them what I thought was my impressive resume. When I didn't get work, I thought that as soon as our family had settled into our new home, the phone would start ringing day and night with job offers from top-level management people who needed a competent salesman or sales manager. I figured this had to be the way God was going to guide my future. It seemed only logical to me that He would put me back into the same field with equal or greater success. I admired God for having such a brilliant plan for our time here in Kansas City. I planned on making lots of money to help support missionaries and feed the poor. With these godly goals in mind, why wouldn't God put me back in sales? I soon found that God had other plans. It took a while to catch on, but eventually, I learned that God's plans for my life are far better than my own!

Immediately after the furniture was in place and the boxes were unpacked, I began to actively seek that perfect job I knew God had waiting. I spent several months interviewing for various sales positions. Each round of interviews went well. In most of the positions I applied for, there were fifty to eighty applicants. I would often be one of the last people considered for the job, but in every situation, someone else would be hired. Although this pattern wore me down emotionally, I continued to interview for sales positions for two years, even though the doors to these types of jobs continued to close.

Then one day, Caryl and I brilliantly decided that maybe God was not leading me into another sales career. The continual rejection of not being hired didn't bother me at first. What bothered me was the response of my friends and family back in Illinois as they started to catch on to the truth that I was having trouble finding a sales job. The people we loved the most began doubting our decision to move to Kansas City.

Caryl began having dreams about people talking about us, doubting we made the right decision because I couldn't get work. In the midst of this external disappointment, Caryl and I had peace. We knew God wanted us to continue living in Missouri. Although circumstances looked bleak, He kept on confirming that we had made the right decision. We truly felt His hand over us, loving us and teaching us through every life experience. We now realize that these were precious days; God had planned each one to lay a solid foundation for the future He had planned for us.

By the spring of 1995, I was desperate for any kind of work, so I applied for a part-time job delivering telephone books. I put thick telephone books into plastic bags, loaded up my car, and drove into the neighborhoods assigned to me. Once the route was done, I'd head back to pick up more telephone books and start another route. This job lasted for several months. I learned some interesting lessons. It was hard at first, but now I can laugh

PROPHETIC TRAINING: IN THE SCHOOL OF HUMILITY

because I know that God was humbling me. Delivering phone books felt far below what I'd been accustomed to.

I'd left a career in Illinois, where everyday life included entertaining customers at fancy restaurants, driving nice cars, wearing expensive clothes, keeping my shoes shined, and walking around with a few hundred dollars in my pocket. Now my pockets were empty, and my shoes were dusty! I had no idea that God had enrolled me in the School of Humility. The tuition is free, but it can cost a lot to graduate. My classroom had no walls, and God was my only teacher. It was lonely at times.

On my first day, I arrived ten minutes early. A lady I'd talked to on the phone told me that I needed to attend the required training session before I could be released as an official telephone book courier. I was insulted. "Training session?" "Official Telephone Book Courier?" I hoped they wouldn't make me wear some type of identification badge. I could see it now. The neighborhood kids asking my children what their dad did for a living. "My dad's an Official Telephone Book Courier. Do you want to see his badge?"

They made me sit through a fifteen-minute video that was produced in the 1950s. All I had to do was throw a telephone book by a person's front porch. *How hard could that be?* As if that wasn't bad enough, at the end of the video they asked me if I had any questions about stuffing a telephone book in a plastic bag. Good grief! I suffered through the training session, gritted my teeth, and endured feelings of embarrassment and humiliation.

After it was over, I met my supervisor. We struck up a conversation and, putting two and two together, I figured out that he was in a worse position than I was. Every morning he caught a ride from one of his friends who dropped him off at what I sarcastically called Telephone Book Headquarters, a one-star motel where the official telephone book couriers gathered every morning to pick up our routes for the day.

God was working to turn me into sweet wine, and I was sour grapes. I resisted His crushing. I saw myself as a highly educated, knowledgeable person, and here I was listening to a man, who I thought needed my help, explain the tricks of the trade for delivering telephone books. Believe it or not, there were rules and regulations to follow. If a telephone book courier broke a rule and was reported to the company manager, he or she would not get paid for that particular route. Some mornings I would show up early, and it was my job to make coffee for him! I was in culture shock and I didn't like it.

My nightly prayers went something like, "God, I thought you moved us to Kansas City to train us in prophetic ministry. I thought you wanted to use me to speak life and encouragement into people. What does delivering telephone books and taking orders from this man have to do with prophecy?"

I began to feel a strange resemblance to Joseph in the dungeon. I remember feeling particularly discouraged one morning. Things were not working out as I'd planned or hoped. I was angry. On one hand, I kind-of-sort-of had a hunch that God was humbling me. He was preparing me by odd jobs that were bruising my ego as well as draining my bank account.

My memory of the day I quit my sales job and how He told me that I would be working for Him stayed with me. After working in a steady job for twelve years, I felt God was changing our course. On my last day of work, I recall sitting in my car in the parking lot a bit stunned. As I was getting ready to leave, I felt the Lord clearly say, "You're working for me now. You're working for me full-time."

On the other hand, I was beginning to think that moving my family to Kansas City had been a mistake. I was also frustrated with God because I thought He was punishing me for some unknown reason. I know this is screwy theology, but it's how I was feeling at the time. Biblically, I know that God loves us and wants the best for us. But being in these circumstances made me feel somehow out of God's will. My life was miserable at best. At this point, absolutely nothing was going right for me.

One morning, as I was in the garage of our duplex putting telephone books into plastic bags, I suddenly realized I wasn't the only one in the garage. It's hard to describe, but I felt a Presence standing in one corner of

PROPHETIC TRAINING: IN THE SCHOOL OF HUMILITY

the garage. I could see the bottom of a brown robe and sandals and someone, standing there, watching me. Without interrupting my rhythm of stuffing books into plastic bags, I turned to look, and I immediately knew it was Jesus.

My emotions were torn between falling on my face in adoration to Him and responding out of my pain and frustration—wanting to know why He had put me in this mess. My true feelings rose up inside me and I said, "What do You want?" As soon as those words were spoken, I knew how terribly wrong that was and that my punishment would be severe. He quickly answered my question by saying, "I've come to be your friend." I thought I was going to faint (really). I was expecting a much different response—something like, "Why are you so upset with me?" or "How dare you talk to me like that!"

Such humility! His response was one of friendship. He overlooked my inappropriate, immature response and quite simply said that He wanted to spend time with me. Imagine that for a moment! God shows up, and the first thing I do is give him a piece of my mind. My advice to you is that when God shows up, try not to have a bad attitude as I did. I'm embarrassed to even think back to that encounter. At the time, **I was too blind to see clearly that God was working on my character. He was giving me priceless lessons about humility and servant leadership. He was teaching me about putting others ahead of myself even when I didn't feel like it. He was grinding me down with opportunities to live out Philippians 2:3:**

> Do nothing out of selfishness ambition or vain conceit, but in humility consider others better than yourselves.

He was starting to teach me His ways. He was doing it in such a way that I didn't even know it! As I've mentioned, my job was my classroom; it was my initial training ground for learning how to be a servant and love others. I had tried to avoid the School of Humility. I wanted to be a servant, but I changed my mind when people start treating me like one.

God's fingerprints were all over my days. I was in the midst of crying out to Him for a greater prophetic anointing, and He was answering me in unusual ways. Some days I would deliver telephone books to mainline denominational churches that do not teach about prophecy. To make my job more interesting, whenever I took a telephone book to a church, I made it a habit to ask to meet with the pastor. I would tell the pastor that my family recently moved from Illinois and that I was looking for a sales job, but in the interim I was making ends meet by delivering telephone books. I would ask him questions about his church, his family, whatever came to mind. I would always end by asking if I could pray for him and his church. Every pastor said yes. We would typically go into his office to pray, and usually God would give me a prophetic word to share with the pastor; he was often taken aback. While these pastors did not teach about prophecy and some were strongly opposed to it, they acknowledged that God was speaking through me. **Prophecy and prayer go hand in hand.** As the years unfold, we have slowly grown into this understanding.

The funny part about the whole thing was that I began coming home at the end of the day with a big smile on my face. At the evening dinner table, I would share with Caryl and our children all the interesting ways in which God had moved on that particular day. Delivering telephone books began to take on a whole new meaning. I began to enjoy getting out of bed each morning, wondering what God was going to do. My highest desire was, and still is, to please and obey Him, regardless of the costs. He knows that, and He was changing my hard heart. He was teaching me, and I was learning to be obedient to Him despite my own feelings and the circumstances I was facing.

One of the stories that I can now look back on and laugh about happened toward the end of my brief career as a telephone book courier. I was working in an upscale area close to a high school about the time school let out for the day. I was walking back to my car when a blue sedan full of students drove by, and in one voice they all yelled at me, "Hey, loser." As you can imagine, this was discouraging. It wasn't that I believed what they said was true, but it did remind me of my present situation. *After all, what successful man in his early thirties goes around delivering telephone books at three o'clock in the afternoon?*

Once the telephone book delivery job was completed, I thought for sure God was going to put me back into a lucrative sales career. I thought, in my own mind, that I had been embarrassed enough, and I wanted God to show me my next career. I wanted a greater challenge. I thought that I was made for much more. My prayers at night continued to be, "Lord, when am I going to learn more about prophecy and hearing Your voice? I learned a lot about humility delivering telephone books; please don't embarrass me anymore. Some of my friends are laughing behind my back. I think I'm ready for a job with a little more excitement and responsibility." Again God answered my prayer in a way that differed from my expectations. . . . Do you see a pattern developing?

A story fits in here—as a family we had many sweet experiences sharing with others in our neighborhood—but this is our over-the-top favorite.

At the time, we felt very poor. The lowest point in our natural life was getting a taste of what it is like to be poor, but that was when God taught us the greatest lesson we have ever experienced. Matthew 5:3 says,

Blessed are the poor in spirit, for theirs is the kingdom of heaven (NKJV).

We learned that we need to be "poor in spirit" to experience the deepest portion of the kingdom of Heaven and that it is a gift to be able to share our hardships with friends going through similar experiences. Many of our friends were like us; we all wanted the greater gifts that God wanted to give us. Together **we learned that being "poor in spirit" isn't always being poor in the natural realm, but in recognizing our need for God, in seeing how it's true poverty to try to live without Him.** In living through our unique times of want, God taught us and gave us a touch of the Kingdom of Heaven promised to the "poor in spirit."

The experience I'm going to tell you was a monumental one in our lives and in the life of our community. It birthed our understanding of prayer and our commitment to pray. God met us in a divine way. In our desperate state, He rained His Holy Spirit over our home and gave us a gift, a supernatural taste of "how good and pleasant it is for brethren to dwell together in unity" (see Psalm 133:1, NKJV).

Water Tower Story

On February 12, 1995, we had an incredible God encounter. After the Sunday morning church service, we decided to go out for pizza with two other families. During our meal, we felt the Lord beckoning us to pray for each other. So after eating, we all went back to our place. As we got settled into talking and praying with our friends, we all felt the spirit of prophecy resting on us in an unusual way. We responded by continuing to prophesy and pray over each other.

Somehow, the news that we were having a supernatural encounter with God traveled quickly through the neighborhood. Friends and friends of friends began filling our home for prayer. It somehow became a magnet of spiritual activity. People were hungry for God and for whatever reason, we felt as if there was an open heaven above us. By early evening, people were waiting outside to come in. Some people were slain in the spirit as they stepped through the door. It was quite a scene! Cars driving by were attracted by the line leading down our driveway, and we soon had strangers and nonbelievers asking for prayer once they came inside our home.

For the next several hours, we huddled in small groups as we prayed for more of what was on God's heart. Our children were praying and travailing alongside us. Each one had received the Lord's burden to pray and intercede for healing, revival, and more of His presence. We asked God for a sign in the natural realm that our prayers had reached Heaven and our prayers were being answered. We prayed and waited.

At about nine o'clock in the evening one of our friends left to go back home and put his children to bed. On his way he witnessed an unusual occurrence and then came back to tell us about it. A valve had burst on a local water tower and water was gushing out from near the top of this huge, several-stories-high reservoir. We believe to this day that through intercession something changed in the spiritual atmosphere. The gushing water was God's sign to us.

That evening, Caryl found that she was made for intercession. This was one of the missing links to the depths of prayer that she so desired to walk in. The Lord introduced Caryl and those in our home to what corporate prayer truly can be. Sometimes we don't know what we are praying for, but He lays those burnings on our hearts so we can partner with Him in prayer. Romans 8:26 says, "We do not know what we ought to pray for, but the Spirit himself intercedes for us with groans that words cannot express."

Around midnight, after everyone had left our house, one of our neighbors called to say he was experiencing a severe headache. His wife was considering taking him into the ER, but first they called me to come over—knowing that prayer had been supernaturally released that evening in our home. Instead of going by myself, I brought another friend of mine, Kirk Bennett. After five or ten minutes of persevering prayer, his headache was gone. When I arrived back home, Caryl said that she felt God's healing presence in our home. We know well that this was not of us but only a bit of God's power that rested on us that day. We wish and pray for this kind of God resting to come again and again in the future.

The next day our daughters and their friend Amy were baking Valentine cookies in our kitchen. While they were baking, the girls talked among themselves. As they shared we listened from the other room. "Don't you love the feeling when the Lord's presence rests in the house? The angels are here with us as we bake these cookies. Isn't this great! Don't you love it?" This power and spirit of prayer rested over us, our home, and our friends for several days.

As I write this chapter, it is January of 2009. We are in the midst of what some would call a global economic meltdown. Through no fault of their own, some readers might feel like failures. Man's measure of success is far different from God's yardstick. Man says that to be successful we need to have status, wealth, and the applause of our boss, but God's Word says this in 1 Samuel 16:7:

Man looks at the outward appearance, but the LORD **looks at the heart.**

Look at what Psalm 24:3-4 says,

Who may ascend the hill of the LORD**? Who may stand in his holy place? He who has clean hands and a pure heart, who does not lift up his soul to an idol or swear by what is false.**

If God asks you to do something, obey Him.

Before we moved to Missouri in 1994, the Lord clearly spoke to me about our calling and said, "The world has no knowledge of what I'm calling you and Caryl into, and even some of your Christian friends won't understand." At the time, I thought I knew exactly what that meant. I was wrong. After fifteen years, we now know that God was speaking to us about the *fasted lifestyle.*

In 1999, Mike Bickle became more intentional about launching the International House of Prayer. He would often call people forward to dedicate themselves to prayer and fasting during ministry time in services. It was in this context that God gave Caryl and me the mandate to live a fasted lifestyle. Simply put, the fasted lifestyle is mostly about prayer, fasting, and extravagant giving. We believe that when we engage in these three activities with intimacy with Jesus, our hearts will grow in love and partnership with God. And because of His love, demonstrated at the Cross, He delights to draw us even closer to Himself. We need to position ourselves before God's desire and delight in us so we can engage in these activities over the long haul in a positive and healthy way. This lifestyle isn't a vow of poverty, but instead it is to offer up a yes in our hearts to live totally surrendered to Him. In that comes the willingness to be placed in the position of dependence on God. This does not line up too well with the American culture. **In our world we are taught to line up our finances, future plans, and to have securities. In the latter days, we won't need our plans and securities. What we will need is the ability to hear God's voice.** The cost then comes by yielding our so-called storybook lives to Him and letting Him be the author.

TWELVE

Stepping up the Ladder

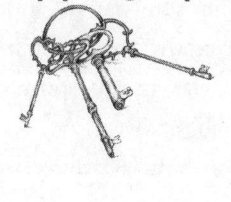

GOD LOVES TO ANSWER His children's prayers, but we have problems when His answers come in ways we don't expect or appreciate. Several days after praying, my neighbor came over and asked me if I'd consider painting his house. We desperately needed the extra money. I was in another round of interviews for a sales job, and the next interview was a week away, so I agreed. Thus, my painting career officially began. As I started painting my friend's house, discouragement settled into my heart. I had graduated from Official Telephone Book Courier to house painter, who arrived home every evening wondering why in the world God would send me to Kansas City to deliver telephone books and paint houses. I felt like I was wasting my time and energy. I was fed up with God, fed up with His church, and I'd had it with all the people who lived in my subdivision. More than once I wanted to be like Dorothy in the *Wizard of Oz* and close my eyes, click my heels, and say, "There's no place like home." I imagined that when I opened my eyes, we'd suddenly find ourselves back in Illinois (and not Kansas City), and I'd again be a successful corporate-level salesman with big bucks in my pockets.

That week was hotter than usual. One day when the heat index was about 122 degrees as I was standing on the roof, trying to paint some trim, the heat reflecting off the shingles was unbearable. The back of my neck had been sunburned for several days; by mid-morning the perspiration was dripping. I had another two or three hours to endure before lunch.

By noon I'd started getting weak and dizzy. I said to myself, *I need to get off this roof and take a rest.* As I looked down at my old gym shoes, I noticed that a part of the soles had melted from the heat on the roof. I went home for lunch crying and laughing at the same time. I was crying because I didn't have enough money to buy another pair of shoes, and my sunburn was killing me. I was laughing about the joy I felt in being obedient to God. What He was requiring of me was, in my opinion, absolutely ridiculous. Despite this, I sensed God's delight over my life. My enthusiasm for painting was zero, and I was still several days away from completing the house. My head was throbbing as Caryl poured a cold drink for me. After lunch, still not feeling that great, I left our air-conditioned house and went back to the heat and paint fumes.

Later that afternoon, I had an impression that someone else in our neighborhood was going to call me about painting their house. I wondered where that thought came from. I quickly dismissed the notion. I was so hot that I thought heat stroke might have altered my thinking processes. I knew that this was not why I moved my family to Kansas City! If I had wanted to be a painter, I could have stayed in Illinois and started a business there. My thoughts were out of control. I was beginning to doubt that I had heard God correctly. *Had I missed it? Should we have stayed in Illinois and NOT moved to Kansas City. Did I miss it by moving? Had I made the biggest mistake of my life by quitting a job that could have made me a rich man someday? Was I the one who had convinced Caryl and our children that God was calling us to move here? What if I had made the wrong choice? Was God mad at me for something?* Questions bombarded me.

That evening I received a phone call from another neighbor asking me to paint her house. *Was it really God who had given me that impression earlier that day?* I reluctantly agreed, and as soon as I finished the first house, I started another one. The first day on the job my ladder broke, and I ended up painting the entire house with a broken ladder. I was a sight. To make matters worse, my ten-year-old daughter, Erin, had to give me ten dollars to buy a paintbrush. Frustrated, dejected, and broke, I told God I was finished painting forever—or so I thought.

The following Sunday during worship time in church, I had a vision of several paintbrushes of different sizes. My sense was that more painting jobs were coming to me. I didn't share this with Caryl right away because I truly did not want to be a painter. I wanted to get back into sales, to make a great income, and to learn more about prophecy and hearing God's voice! I did not want to disappoint her with the news that her husband had been demoted to a painter with a broken ladder and no tools.

Caryl, however, was always encouraging me to go over God's promises to us and not to become discouraged. She was the glue that held our family together. I have said this publicly hundreds of times. Caryl has a gift of faith that amazes me.

While I was wondering why God was torturing me like this, He was teaching me that He will always help me. In His school of character development there are no shortcuts. In case you skipped over that last sentence let me repeat myself—**in God's school of character development there are no shortcuts. We must pass every test before going on to the next lesson. The good news is that God is right there beside us. He is more interested in character and integrity than He is in ministry or gifting. If we forget this, it is easy to get frustrated and discouraged and quit before the finish line. God promises that He will be with us on each and every step of our journey**. I am here to tell you that He keeps His promise. Not only has He kept His promise to us, but our family has been blessed beyond our wildest dreams.

Several days after finishing my second painting job, another friend drove over to see us. He'd heard that I was painting houses that summer and his needed doing, so he asked if I wanted to give him an estimate. Inside I was furious! *How dare God give me another house to paint when all I wanted was a sales job?* I said to my friend, "I'm not really a painter. I'm actually looking for a sales job, and I'm sure it's just around the corner."

I tried to discourage him, but he gently pressed me and said he'd still like an estimate. I joked and said, "The only way I'll paint your house is if the quote I give you exactly matches the amount you're willing to spend." I thought for sure that there would be no way on earth for my estimate to match his budget that precisely. I'm not sure what the odds were, but in my mind it was a million-to-one shot. I told him I wouldn't even look at his house but would pray, and God would tell me what to charge him.

The next day I presented my bid. It was the exact amount he and his wife had decided to spend. My friend was stunned. So was I! *How could this be? Had God tricked me into this? He told me the amount to charge, but didn't He understand that all I wanted to do was get a sales job and live a normal life?*

So I painted his house. During the last week I worked there, I saw a vision relating to their three daughters. When the painting was finished, I shared it with them. It was about 1 Corinthians 13:13, and each of his daughters would have faith, hope, and love. In other words, the oldest daughter would have the gift of faith, the next would be filled with hope, and the youngest would love unconditionally.

If I hadn't been so full of my own thoughts, I might have begun to see that as I obeyed God, He was training me to hear His voice. He was answering my prayers and using me in the marketplace of life, but I was fighting with Him and trying to wiggle out of where He wanted me to be and what he wanted me to do. That was not a good idea! We should always go where God is leading.

I suffered another setback when I took the postal exam. When I saw an ad in the paper stating when it would be offered in Kansas City, I told Caryl that I was more than certain I could pass the test with flying colors and get a job delivering mail. *All I had to do was take a test, right?* I smugly figured my high intellectual abilities would surely help me. In my pride and arrogance I thought, *How hard could a postal exam be?* I wondered if I would be the first person to get a perfect score. I was geared up and ready. I even told our own postal carrier that I was taking the test.

On the day of the test, I drove downtown to Kansas City. It was crowded when I arrived. The line of people wrapped around the outside of the building. I could not believe how many people had an interest in the postal exam. I finished the test and drove home quite confidently. I honestly thought I'd score 100 percent. I walked in and confidently told Caryl how well I had done.

Several weeks passed before my score came in the mail. I opened up the envelope and almost fainted when I realized that I had flunked. *How could this be? Was this another one of God's plans to discourage me? Was He torturing me?* Evidently, I had put the correct answers in the wrong boxes on the answer sheet. When I read question fifteen, I put the answer in box sixteen. My score was so low that's the only way I could have done so poorly. To make matters worse, the next day our mail carrier asked me how I had done on the test. I told her what my score was, and she thought I was joking and started to laugh. I assured her it was no joke, and that I had in fact flunked the test. You should have seen the look on her face!

THIRTEEN

Another Demotion?

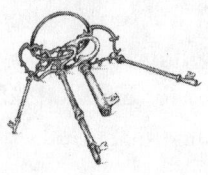

I LEARNED SLOWLY; I thought that once I'd stopped delivering telephone books and finished painting a few duplexes, that God would surely promote me into stable work that offered obvious eternal benefits and rewards. I thought I had suffered enough. **I was confident that something had to change and had no idea it was me that needed to change.** I prayed that I would embrace "all that God had for me." How many of you know that is a dangerous prayer to pray?

In the mode of embracing all that God wanted for us, we found ourselves battling the abnormality of quietness. The quietness I'm referring to is too much time on our hands. In our culture, unproductive, empty time seems wasteful. Allowing it feels like giving our days up to something wrong. Somehow, Caryl and I knew that in the empty, quiet times the Lord was developing a contemplative lifestyle. He was teaching us about the life He planned for us. In this new place of solitude and stillness, we were learning how to hear His soft voice. We were desperate to know Him deeply as we knew He was our provision. We prayed for His provision daily. On most days our situation looked bleak, and many times He answered our prayers at the last minute. We didn't know what would be ahead—how we would have food for the next week.

Before one evening meal, as we thanked God for our food, it dawned on Caryl and me that for the first time in our lives we really knew what it meant to be thankful for our daily bread. We were beginning to understand what Jesus meant when He taught His disciples to pray, "Give us this day our daily bread." Once again we found ourselves crying in front of our children in complete humility. It doesn't feel too good on the outside, but on the inside we felt the sweetness of the Lord—we always have at such times. To Caryl and me, thanking the Father for our food that night was a golden moment. We wouldn't trade it for anything. God's blessings are precious. We were learning lessons that many Americans never learn, that our God is a faithful provider, and when He meets our simple needs, we receive one of the greatest rewards in all the earth.

During that season our spiritual mentor was Jim Gochenour. I found myself continually running to his front doorstep hoping he could drop a few nuggets of hope into my being. Jim was the ultimate example of a servant. He never turned me away or gave me any inclination that I was a nuisance. Having a spiritual father who was consistently available was an incredible gift to us.

Every Friday evening we met with Jim, his wife Joyce, and a core of others for a weekly prophetic nurture group. All Jim and Joyce would do was love and receive us. They taught us how to listen and hear the Holy Spirit by modeling it. The Lord spoke prophetically through them. Encouragement echoed throughout their home. Caryl and I would often come feeling discouraged and always leave filled and energized.

Week after week we walked away with the message to hang in with what the Lord was revealing to us—even though it was an abstract way of life to us, one without familiar concrete reference points, a paradigm we couldn't yet grasp. During the week, when I was in desperation, Jim would take a moment to hear me; then he would remind me to go back and continue to obey—no matter how bizarre it might seem to me. It actually was quite simple. I needed to seek the Lord and then do what He told me to do for that day. Most of the time He told me to just spend my time with our children and Caryl. Sometimes I was even told to go to the swimming pool with the kids. I was learning that I didn't have to strive to make an income. All I needed to do was trust and obey, then He would provide.

Caryl and I also found a community of friends in our neighborhood. At that time, some of our friends were in a spot like ours. We wondered, *How does life work for us when God is calling us to follow Him, and we have families to provide for?* We met regularly, seeking God, wanting to please Him and wanting be godly leaders in our families. We invested time in our relationships and in making memories with our children. Our kids knew this time in their lives was very special. Children are sensitive and actually love it when God softens their fathers' hearts.

Suddenly, things changed again—with an unexpected turn. But, as usual, not in the way I had expected! (Do you see the pattern continuing?) The Lord had been teaching me that I could count on what He said: if He told me something would happen, then it clearly would. He had told me about many painting jobs before I got them, but one fine day, that came to a halt. A new season began. There were no more clues for the next several months. He was trusting me with silence. I was trying to be productive in my time without work and was learning about the contemplative life when one day I heard God say, "You'll be again, soon." About another two weeks went by and sure enough a contractor called me on the phone needing help. I jumped at the opportunity and began working the next day. Over the years, we have learned that God's timing is always perfect.

So, in the fall of 1995 God sent me back to work again. My foreman wasn't the most ethical man in the world, but I needed the job, so I figured I could endure it for a season. The construction crew consisted of one teenager, three old-timers and yours truly! Suffice it to say that these men were all into machismo. I was at the bottom of the pecking order so they treated me rather rudely at the beginning. After a few weeks on the job they realized that I was going to stay for a while and started being nicer. As best I could, I was trying to be salt and light.

At first, I didn't say anything to let them know I was a Christian, but it quickly became evident that my lifestyle was very different from theirs. I came to enjoy working with them. They were lost and needed a Savior. I wanted to be faithful where God placed me. It was such a marked contrast to my sales days in Illinois: there were no more suit coats, no more cell phones, no more walking around with three hundred dollars in my pockets. Instead, I was climbing scaffolding, or sanding base boards on my hands and knees most of the day. I sanded so much that my fingertips became raw; they would crack open and bleed. To remedy this, I would tape my fingers before I started working each day. Not only was this painful, it was embarrassing as well. This was another new learning experience for me.

These people mattered to Jesus. God was allowing me, or rather giving me, the opportunity to love on them unconditionally. I was constantly reminded how greatly His grace and mercy are needed in all of our lives. Jesus began to change my heart towards them, to give me His heart for them, and I began praying for them. Slowly, they were becoming friends. I would tell them at lunch breaks how there was a God in Heaven who was madly in love with them. At first, my words were met with rounds of laughter and dismay. After a while, God began softening their hearts. During breaks they would end up coming to me, and we'd talk about the problems in their lives. Sometimes the others would listen. This was frontline Christianity. I loved it.

I remember the day one of the men came up to me and started to share how a friend was getting on his nerves. He asked me for advice. I really had to lean into the Holy Spirit because as best I could I wanted to reflect Christ's love at every opportunity. He listened to every word I said and knew that he needed to make changes.

Another day I began to feel a prophetic spirit come on me. At first, I tried to resist it because it seemed like an odd time for the Lord to want me to speak to them. I wasn't exactly in a spiritual mood when I felt God's hand touch me that particular day. He began giving me specific things to tell each man. I knew the words were to be shared that very day; it was quite unlike other occasions when I prayed for God's timing. So, out of obedience, I began talking individually to each man.

They were all impacted. Many of God's words were so deeply personal to these men that they were taken back by them. It was similar to the way I'd been taken back by God's words to me at the Evanston Vineyard. One of the men asked me if it was New Age or ESP. I quickly assured them all that everything I shared was from God. Then, although it had never happened to me before, a preaching anointing came on me for three or four minutes. I was right in the middle of prophetic evangelism telling them of Jesus. At the time, I didn't even know what prophetic evangelism was.

When God sent me into this work, I has been scared and insecure. I feared that He would keep me there, that I would be stuck. I asked myself, *How long will this lesson last?* I felt it was a dead end, that God wasn't going to move me on again.

While there it enlightened my life to be used in such an eternal way. When it was time to leave I was sad, and wished I'd had the honor of leading each man to the Lord. I'd grown to love these men I had worked alongside. All too soon the Lord clearly intervened and told me to get out from under this authority. I knew it was time to obey God's voice again, but I didn't understand His timing.

At the same time as the Lord directed me to leave this job, He also nudged me to buy a van. I qualified for a loan because I hadn't quit yet, but it didn't seem logical to quit and buy a van at the same time. *How could I afford the payment?*

We were pulled two ways. I knew we needed to follow the track of faith we were on, so Caryl and I determined to buy the van even though we knew I had to quit my work at nearly the same time. But we feared presumption. The longer I put off looking for a van, the more intensely I felt disobedient by not buying one. Does that seem strange to you? It did to me. Caryl's advice was, "Let's go look for a van." It sounded like good advice to me, so off we went to a local car dealership. We looked around the car lot for less than an hour and found a van we liked. *This is way too easy,* I thought, *—besides, the salesman is probably going to try to take advantage of my inexperience.* So I told the salesman that I didn't see a van I liked and that I was going to shop around. But as Caryl and I got in the car, I told her I liked the white one with blue stripes. That was the one she liked too. Since I didn't want to jump into the decision, we waited and went back to the dealership when it was closed on a Sunday evening with our children. We could look without being pressured.

After praying about our decision, we really felt God wanted us to purchase it. Our car payment was something like $350 a month. I honestly had no idea how we would make the monthly payments, but I believed that God had put it on my heart to obey and trust Him more. I quit work for the contractor and drove away from the car dealer with a minivan the same Memorial Day weekend. Caryl and I knew this was another offense to the natural mind. We hadn't been brought up to take risks like this. We'd been taught to logically think through our big decisions and not act until all the pieces lined up.

Throughout this time, we sought counsel from our nurture group and found refuge with them. They prayed for and encouraged us through each step God asked us to take. The nurture group helped us confirm that God was, in fact, asking me to quit my job. Actually, God had told me that Memorial Day was going to be my last day at work and just as He'd said, it was! I never missed a van payment, and I'm still driving it, fourteen years later. Right now I use it as my painting van. It's all rusty and dented up, and it has over 235,000 miles on it!

Looking back, we understand the urgency I felt about buying a new vehicle. In 1994, we moved to Kansas City in a small Pontiac Grand Am. By 1996 the children had grown, and with our golden retriever, we could not all fit into the car. The Lord was getting us ready for traveling, not only for family vacations, but also for a ministry that we didn't know was ahead.

FOURTEEN

Praiseworthy Painting

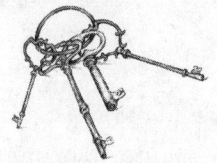

OUR OWN DETERMINATION didn't get us very far. As the summer began, I found myself with a new van with nice big contractor signs on the doors, a car payment, and no jobs! We thought that since we had promptly obeyed God's voice and bought the van, even though it seemed foolish to us, that He would answer us immediately. We waited and waited for God to open a big door, but it stayed closed.

We deliberately chose a name for our new painting business that voiced praise. The signs on the van read Praiseworthy Painting. **We did not feel like praising Him at that moment, but we knew in our hearts that in faith we would be praising the Lord in days to come when we got the full understanding of what this was all about.** This was our faith challenge. We picked Philippians 4:8 for our theme:

> Finally, brethren, whatever things are true, whatever things are noble, whatever things are just, whatever things are pure,

whatever things are lovely, whatever things are of good report, if there is any virtue and if there is anything praiseworthy, meditate on these things (NKJV).

One afternoon, while we were seeking a sign from the Lord—asking Him for a tangible marker for our future, we set out for a drive. Our new Praiseworthy signs were magnetically adhered to the passenger's and driver's doors. By the time we got home, they were missing. Somewhere along the road the signs had blown off and were totally destroyed. We retraced our route and found them on the shoulder of the road, all ripped and torn. Evidently, when they blew off, the traffic behind us had driven over them.

This was not the kind of sign we were looking for. Maybe it was silly to pray for a sign when we knew, deep in our spirits, that God was teaching us to trust Him. We needed to trust, and to wait, and to not be anxious.

Be anxious for nothing, but in everything by prayer and supplication, with thanksgiving, let your requests be made known to God; and the peace of God, which surpasses all understanding, will guard your hearts and minds through Christ Jesus. (Philippians 4:6-7, NKJV)

Our name from Philippians 4:8, seemed to give us grace to not try to understand. We accepted. We didn't need a sign; we just needed God's Word to meditate on.

Little by little, the pieces came together. My father called me on the phone and asked me if I was planning to start a painting business and work at it full-time. I thought he was going to make some sly remark about how our move to Kansas City wasn't working out exactly as planned or that I was wasting my college degree by becoming a painter. But instead, he was very understanding and supportive. His response took me totally by surprise. He said that he was supporting me, whatever new career path I chose. It was a great example of the Father's blessing being poured out on me. He asked me if he could buy some of the painting equipment needed to get me started. I couldn't believe what my ears were hearing. My father was giving me his blessing and believing in my decisions.

Since I was still relatively new at painting and hadn't built up a customer base, when the time came for our family's annual summer vacation, it all seemed very different to us. We always went to Wisconsin in the summer to my in-laws' summer home. My first trip with Caryl and her parents to Door County was right after my senior year in high school. After our marriage we hadn't missed a year, that is, until 1995. We were determined not to miss another family vacation. It had left us feeling as if we had missed Christmas. It had been really sad for all of us. But now, I couldn't leave. I was waiting for two or three painting estimates. No clue had been given to help us anticipate how different this new season would be.

Just before Caryl and the children left me in Kansas, and headed for Door County, we attended Metro's annual summer conference. As we scanned the auditorium for a friend of ours, we noticed several people we knew from Illinois. Caryl and I wondered, *How did they find out about this conference? Metro in Missouri is free flowing in the gifts of the Holy Spirit, and their church in Illinois isn't!*

We went up to one of the men and said, "Aren't you George?" Caryl had been in a ladies' home group for seven years with George's wife, Jan. It was a sweet connection as we told George about our move to Kansas City and our family's new spiritual journey. We quickly found out how hungry George was for the Holy Spirit. He was intrigued and curious about our life and wanted to hear more of our story. He ended up asking me if I would consider driving to Illinois after the conference to paint his house. He figured he could hit two birds with one stone. I could paint his house, and he could ask more in-depth questions about what exactly had prompted our move to Kansas City. He was desperate for more of God.

During the conference itself, it thrilled us to see how the Lord connected the dots and brought us back to the very people we had left. Caryl and I were privileged to watch the Holy Spirit come with answers as we prayed for several men from our old neck of the woods. As soon as the conference was over, our family drove to Jan and George's house in our new van. This was our first road trip. The next day, Caryl drove up to Wisconsin with our children while I stayed and painted George's house.

As I painted, George and I were carried into long discussions about prophecy and hearing God's voice. As best I could, I explained to George that the main reason we moved to Kansas City was to learn more about prophecy and to understand the spiritual gifts that God had given to us. George and Jan were very eager to find this dimension of God. They were so excited that one of the very first nights, after a full day of painting, they called a meeting with their favorite friends—men and women who were also desperate and hungry for more intimacy with Jesus. Our traveling ministry had begun. Although Caryl wasn't there in person, she was praying for me all along the way.

House painting moved us into a place where God could send us to people who didn't know anything about the Holy Spirit or hearing God's voice. "The Spirit of the LORD GOD is upon Me, because the LORD has anointed Me to preach good tidings." Isaiah 61:1 (NKJV). We really didn't have to do much; the Spirit of the Lord moved on the people.

At this first meeting we worshiped, and then the Spirit of the Lord began to guide us in prophecy. God wanted us to be His spokespersons, models to others of following the leading of the Holy Spirit as His revelation came to bless each individual.

Therefore, I remind you to stir up the gift of God which is in you through the laying on of my hands (2 Timothy 1:6, NKJV).

Jan and George's invitation was the kickoff for many more to come. They were the first to host these meetings, and others would follow as time went on. The way God worked reminded us of how He spread the message back in Jesus' time. People experienced the ministry of Jesus, told their friends, and the news spread. We felt a bit like the forerunner, John the Baptist, pointing people to Jesus as we invited the Holy Spirit and watched Him point them to the lovely Son of God. It wasn't about us. It was and is all about God's gracious plan to send out ambassadors to proclaim His good news. As Isaiah prophesied, "The LORD has anointed Me to preach good tidings." This Me is really Us, all of us who are filled with the Holy Spirit. We are all called to be ministers of His Spirit. His Spirit, this excellent gift of the third person of the Godhead, is one way He honors us as His beloved children. The Holy Spirit is our friend. We wondered at His goodness—watching meetings unfold before us for the next several months—and now the months have become years as God so graciously continues to bring His presence to us.

We're grateful for George and Jan and all the point people who hosted the first meetings in Illinois. With no effort on our part, invitations came from other families. When Mike and Kathy Barry eagerly opened their doors to the invitation to the Holy Spirit, many people came and many lives were turned inside out for Jesus—literally changed. Then Dave and Dawn Mitchell's hearts were filled with enthusiasm to hold meetings at their home. These families were the early pioneers who saw the value and impact that prophetic ministry can have. Later on, other families caught the vision as well and hosted meetings. Jesus was always the center of these meetings. As His people ministered to Him, every meeting always came back to Jesus' heart to minister to His people. It was His appointed time to introduce these love hungry worshippers to the Holy Spirit, and it was truly thrilling and praiseworthy.

Come, all you who are thirsty, come to the waters; and you who have no money, come, buy and eat! Come, buy wine and milk without money and without cost (Isaiah 55:1).

Because of painting jobs and ministry invitations, Caryl and I found ourselves traveling in our white minivan practically all summer. God was very good to us that summer, starting a new business, sending us into His ministry, and opening our eyes to more of His ways.

Once again, we were slow to catch on. One day, driving along on a road outside of Milwaukee, Wisconsin, our eyes were opened to see what God had been doing. It finally dawned on us that Praiseworthy was not just a painting business, it was a ministry. We realized that house painting was the vehicle God had given us to do His work. We reminisced about how the Lord spoke to me on my last day as a salesman, remembering how, as I took off my tie and stepped into the parking lot for the last time, the Lord spoke to my heart, "You will work for me now."

As we drove along, the reality of His purpose began to take form in our understanding. We'd already learned to keep moving ahead, not to stop moving forward when we didn't understand what was going on. But that day, Caryl and I experienced what it was to "behold a work of God," to see a plan that He had formulated days and years ahead of us. How amazing is the God we serve! Can you imagine the day in Heaven when every single event in our life will take understandable form? Doesn't it say in the Word that every good work will be rewarded? That day we had a mountain-top experience as we realized the results of walking in faith. We knew for ourselves that faith does have a wonderful reward.

As we ministered to different groups, people began asking us who to make out the honorarium checks to. At first, I wasn't even sure what an honorarium check was. It seemed strange that people would want to pay us to tell our testimony or pray for them. Fortunately, about this time Jim Goll came into our lives and helped us get organized. Jim slowly began to explain to us that we needed to form a ministry, but perhaps I'm getting ahead of the story.

FIFTEEN

A Word of Caution

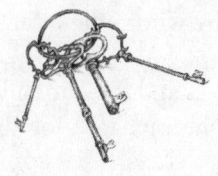

EVEN THOUGH OUR MOVE TO KANSAS CITY looked odd, we knew in our hearts that God was leading us. If we'd listened to Christian friends who tried to talk us out of moving, we wouldn't have moved. People did, in fact, doubt us, which makes discernment vital in any relocation or job change. The enemy is in the business of messing with our minds. Instead of being built up in our faith through significant others we had to stand strong alone with God's Word. His Word in us set our minds free and brought us peace.

> **You will keep him in perfect peace, whose mind is stayed on You, because he trusts in You** (Isaiah 26:3, NKJV).

Our biggest battles weren't with being misunderstood or lack of support, but with the lies that attacked our minds with doubt.

God blesses some people with outwardly conventional lives and sends others on unconventional journeys with Him. We understand now His purpose in this for our unique lives, but while we were walking it out, it was a spiritual workout. In the midst of the adventures God sometimes takes people through, He challenges them to obey and follow to reflect a lifestyle that is out of the ordinary. This can seem odd to people on the outside looking in. Our lives have seemed to model this offense, but then look at the life of Christ. As much as Caryl and I complained, we now can see we are honored ones. What a joy and privilege to have this type of lifestyle. It is a great gift from Heaven to be trusted to prepare the way for Christ's second coming. Many are called to this in the latter days. It says in Matthew 18:7 (NKJV), "Woe to the world because of offenses! For offenses must come, but woe to that man by whom the offense comes!" Matthew 11:6 (NKJV) says, "And blessed is he who is not offended because of Me." This is one of our prayers for ourselves and for our children and grandchildren—that we can understand and be prepared for the offenses that will come in the latter days.

I don't recommend the unusual path God invited our family to walk to anyone! I believe He has a different path set up for each and every one of us. **We all have unique callings and gifts, and God custom makes each path. Problems arise when we try to walk on someone else's path. Problems also occur when we try to run when God is asking us to walk. We need to stay in step with Jesus and walk with Him.**

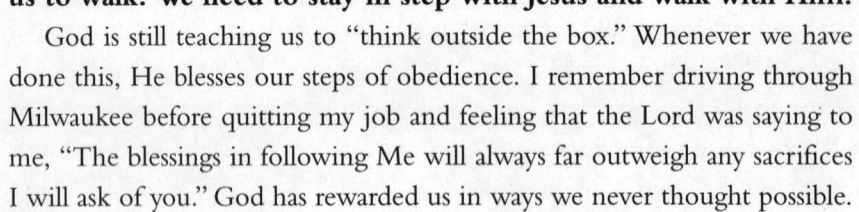

God is still teaching us to "think outside the box." Whenever we have done this, He blesses our steps of obedience. I remember driving through Milwaukee before quitting my job and feeling that the Lord was saying to me, "The blessings in following Me will always far outweigh any sacrifices I will ask of you." God has rewarded us in ways we never thought possible.

SIXTEEN

Blessings As a Result of Obedience

OVER THE YEARS and especially since we've been in ministry, God has given us too many blessings to list. I'll highlight a few in gratitude. If God can bless us this way, I know He can do the same for you.

Blessings for Our Children

Before moving to Kansas City, Caryl and I prayed, more than anything else, for the best place for our children to grow up spiritually. We knew we could be flexible and adapt to just about any living situation, but we wanted our move to benefit LeAnn, Erin, and Brendan. We prayed that our children would have fiery hearts for Jesus, and we knew that role models are key to installing that desire in their hearts.

The Lord is good. He answers our prayers according to our needs. He graciously surrounded our children with people of deep character and zealous spirits, people who could discern the difference between fool's gold and the real stuff.

During their high-school years, perhaps the biggest influence on their lives came from being around young adults who were sold out to Jesus. The Youth Leaders at our church impacted them beyond description. They sealed the deposits of truth we'd been privileged to put into our children and became their friends, cheering them on to build their lives on foundations of purity and honor to the Lord. Solid youth leaders took Brendan under their wings and helped him step out in leadership.

After high school, they became part of Master's Commission, Metro's program for young adults. Young people between the ages of eighteen and twenty-five enrolled in the program after high school. If accepted, they lived with a host family from Metro. Our children were surrounded with young lives on fire for God and grew up spiritually as a result. As each of our daughters enrolled in the program and left our home for a year of growing in God, we were honored to have another student live with us. It was a gift to see our home become an extension of ministry to these girls and to make many new friends. Our son, Brendan, feasted off the godly environment we live in. At every turn, we received far more than we gave. Our children were stretched and challenged to become leaders. They are not ashamed of their faith and step up to the plate as Christians.

Never, not for one second, did we ever want to move to Kansas City to start a ministry or to meet and receive ministry from seasoned prophetic people. We wanted more of God for our entire family; we wanted a place with opportunities for our children to grow and mature in the Lord. God more than answered our prayers; we have seen His hand upon our children's lives. They have been privileged to meet and share their lives with wonderful friends who helped them grow and mature in God.

Our children have also learned to be friends to one another. As parents, we are grateful. God more than answered our prayers. This unique place where we brought our children to grow up was rich, fertile soil for them. It has been fun to watch them grow in every way—mentally, physically, socially, morally, spiritually—you name it, God has provided abundant nurture for them here.

We've come to believe that Kansas City is ordained by God as a melting pot environment, a hot place where His Spirit can flow. We don't know why. Perhaps we are building on the heritage of the pioneers of faith who came before us. Kansas City is known historically as the crossroads to the West.

Financial Blessings

During the embryonic stages of our ministry, God led a family to help us with a substantial monthly gift for eighteen consecutive months. This blessing sustained us; it was of crucial importance as God began to send us out to minister. We could not have done it without their help. We've told them countless times how thankful we are for their extreme generosity. During the early years, other families also blessed us financially. It was a critical time, and the gracious generosity of these families allowed us to continue in ministry. Although there is probably more than one reason God led these particular families to support us, we know that He put them into our lives for a reason. Let me explain why.

Many ministry trips in the early days actually put us back financially. Sometimes we would spend four hundred dollars in traveling expenses to hold a meeting in another city and get seventy-six dollars in the offering! The people loved our ministry, but many figured that since I had a painting job back in Missouri, they did not need to cover our travel expenses or give us any honorarium. We also ran into a few people who had read about supernaturally sustained ministries and thought that God should be our direct supply on a continual basis. In my inexperience, I didn't know how to tell them about our financial needs or to teach them about the scriptural principle of the workman being worthy of wages.

We had several people comment to us, "If your new ministry is really from God, then He will support you." These people had a wait-and-see attitude. In another words, they would not support us unless we seemed to be a *successful* ministry. Since we were just beginning, it was difficult for some people to get behind us financially. Those days are behind us now.

But in the early days, I had no track record to fall back on. We were new to ministry and didn't know what to ask for or how to talk about our expectations or needs. All our hearts wanted was to serve through our prophetic gifting. God provided the finances, teaching us as we went. We have learned how to build relationships and be intentional about asking friends to help support us. We've grown in our ability to be open about finances. Several years into our traveling ministry, IHOP began to have seminars on how to raise support is godly ways. These seminars supplemented what we were already doing and provided us with an opportunity to learn more effective ways to communicate our needs.

The Blessing of God's Generosity

Another blessing was a brand new 1998 Dodge Ram Van. The family who gave it to us wanted us to have a dependable car for ministry trips. Our family will never forget the day that we received this gift. We were visiting friends in another state and they invited us over for breakfast. After breakfast, they led us outside. To our surprise, we saw a new van in their driveway. Before we knew it, our kids had jumped inside and I was thrown the keys. Caryl and I stared at each other in disbelief for what seemed like several minutes. We were overwhelmed to say the least.

Over the years we have been given many gifts—money, a new washing machine, furniture, carpeting, computers, and a refrigerator. These tokens from God have greatly encouraged us. Many gifts were delivered just as the needs arose. Every year, generous giving covered all our homeschooling materials. Our children were also able to take ministry trips. LeAnn and Erin went to Guatemala in 1999 and Erin and Brendan went to Nicaragua with their youth group in 2001. Visiting a third-world country and seeing the benefits of bringing Jesus to people through service and love has changed them forever.

Another gift was a cell phone. Many years ago Caryl and I were praying about getting one, but it seemed to be an extravagant purchase, so we decided to wait and asked God to provide a way for us to buy one. Several days later we received a letter from a friend saying that she felt God wanted her to send us fifty dollars for a special gift, something we wanted to buy but weren't sure we could afford. Wow. God answered that prayer fast—the cell phone cost exactly fifty dollars!

Another time we wanted to fly to Illinois during the Christmas holidays to see our families. The tickets were expensive, but we felt peace about purchasing them. Just before we left, we received a letter from a friend saying, "Dear John and Caryl, We decided to sell some stocks that we had from work. The day we decided to sell the stock, it went up almost four dollars a share. We decided that the Lord wanted us to share the blessing with you." Enclosed was a check for $850, enough to cover our airfare to Chicago. It was so exciting to call our friends and thank them.

One particular morning, Caryl woke up early to intercede for our finances. As she was praying, the Lord showed her a light gleaming through our door frame. In reality, the door was sealed shut in the darkness of the early morning. Later that morning, after working on this very book, Caryl and I wanted to pray again about finances. Just as we began praying, we heard the doorbell ring. I went upstairs to greet a friend of ours. He said that earlier that morning he and his wife both felt prompted to drop a check off for us. I thanked him and walked back downstairs to tell Caryl. I handed her the check, and we both sat there for a moment shaking our heads. God had impressed it upon our friends to drop off the check before we had started to pray! In that moment, God seemed very close to us. We prayed and His answer came in less than a minute! It doesn't always happen like that, but when it does, it really lifts our faith.

Two incredible times we were instantly delivered from financial debt through gifts and twice the IRS helped us because they made a mistake on our taxes.

Now if we had been living in presumption, unwilling to work, and **expecting people to help us out and meet our needs, it is likely that our difficulties would have increased; God would not have answered our prayers with such incredible kindness. We were truly seeking Him and wanting to obey Him, wanting to learn His ways**

of faith. I think we were where He wanted us to be and doing what He wanted us to be doing. I'm just saying this as a caution for people who might want to follow our path without God specifically calling them to it.

And I don't want it to sound as if money is mailed to us everyday. It isn't. We've had difficult times, but we've remembered what Paul said in Philippians 4:12-13:

> I know what it is to be in need, and I know what it is to have plenty. I have learned the secret of being content in any and every situation, whether well fed or hungry, whether living in plenty or in want. I can do everything through him who gives me strength.

The Blessing of Trust

In the past fifteen years, we have experienced the ebbs and flows of ministry and work. Some years we've ministered more than we worked in the marketplace. During those seasons, we received more financial support. Conversely, there have been three or four consecutive years with hardly any ministry when both Caryl and I worked to provide for our family. Never once did we have a mindset that expected people to support us. We never wanted to become dependent on others' giving to us.

Over the years, we've seen some in ministry who develop an expectation of others giving to them. They receive as if it were a right or entitlement. We never wanted to follow this example for our family. Paul's example of tent making is far more honorable, for it keeps the givers and potential givers from stumbling and keeps the lines clear between giving, receiving, and the presumption of taking.

The bottom line is that God always knows our needs. He supplies and sustains us along our journeys. We can look back and see how God has our best interests at heart in everything He does for us.

SEVENTEEN

Forerunners

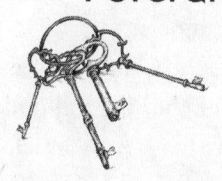

WHEN WE FIRST BEGAN hearing the words "forerunners" and "forerunner ministry" we did not understand their full meaning. We are growing in our understanding of these terms and will explain briefly to help put this last chapter into perspective.

A great biblical example of a forerunner is John the Baptist. His ministry was about preparing people for the Messiah. In John 3:28 we read, "You yourselves can testify that I said, 'I am not the Christ but am sent ahead of him.'" John was always pointing to Jesus. His ministry was to teach repentance and ready God's people for the coming Christ. Successful ministry is about putting the focus on God's name and promoting what is on His heart instead of trying to make our ministry "look good" (see John 3:30).

Forerunners prepare the way by preparing the way for Jesus' return. We read in Isaiah 40:3, "A voice of one calling: 'In the desert prepare the way for the LORD; make straight in the wilderness a highway for our God.'" They are messengers who proclaim and sometimes even live out, in their personal lives, things that many others will experience in the future. At times they look a bit out of step because they are a step or two ahead of what God is about to do in the earth. Through their own lives and message, God prepares forerunners to help others understand the times and seasons, to see what Jesus is doing and respond to Him.

Forerunners are also messengers within their spheres of influence. In some sense, as we respond to God's unique and creative initiatives and follow Him to fulfill our destinies, we all become forerunners. You do not have to be a pastor or in full-time ministry to carry a forerunner message. Intercessors can be forerunner messengers. Artists and musicians, businessmen and homemakers are also forerunners.

Thirty-three years ago, on the night Caryl and I met, God gave Caryl a glimpse of our future without giving her the full understanding. He gave her an invitation that made her heart burn with anticipation and deposited faith and the desire to pray our ministry into maturity. We did not know God was putting us on a path to be forerunners, but it began to unfold as we stepped out in faith. God put His desire in us, and we began praying and seeking Him, trying to gain a fuller understanding of what being a forerunner meant. We have been walking in faith and have been in training. Now, at this moment in time, we sense that God is calling us to step into the place that He designed for us. Let me explain how God visited me to redirect the course of our lives.

May 2008 — Front Room Visitation

One night I went to bed, especially discouraged about my life and, quite frankly, a little frustrated with God. I don't remember saying a whole lot to Caryl as I slipped under the covers. I let out a sigh and rolled over, pulling the pillow over my head. My discouragement and frustration stemmed from my seeming inability to be successful on support-raising trips to Illinois and Michigan in the prior months, the wrong perception that there was no fruit in my life, and an overall dissatisfaction with where I was in my life. All this was making me miserable. I "suffered in silence" as I tried to fall asleep. In some ways, I felt like Charlie Brown when his friends used to yell at him and he would walk away dejected with his head down. From my vantage point, things were not going my way. Can some of you relate to this?

I dozed off to sleep only to be awakened by a heavenly presence in our bedroom. Caryl was still sleeping, and I did not want to wake her. Initially, I wasn't sure if I was dreaming or not. After a few seconds of trying to orient myself in the dark, I suddenly had a vision that the Lord was out in our front room sitting in my favorite chair. It was now apparent to me that I was not dreaming, but was at the beginning of a heavenly visitation.

This might seem almost incomprehensible to you, but I was still discouraged after I woke up. So I told the Lord that I was upset with Him and I wanted to be left alone. I know it's difficult to imagine that was my response, but it was. I rolled over, and the last thing I remember was a gold box that He left on the floor near my chair before He vanished.

When I woke up the next morning, Caryl asked me if I had dreamt the night before. This was not unusual because we asked each other this on a regular basis. I responded with no, but then I told her that the Lord appeared to me in a vision in the front room. Her eyes opened wide, and she asked, "Did you get up to see what He wanted?" No, I confessed sheepishly. She absolutely could not believe what I had just said. She firmly yet gently told me how most people yearn for a heavenly visit—and when it happened to me, I squandered the opportunity because I was frustrated with God. Several minutes later, I realized that I'd forgotten to tell Caryl that Jesus left a gold box on the floor before He left. She asked me, "What was in the box?" I said, "I don't know. He left before I could ask Him." Perhaps getting a bit frustrated with me in the midst of my pity party Caryl said, "Pray today that Jesus will return and show you what was in the gold box." "That's a great idea," I muttered, feeling rather embarrassed. So before going to bed the following evening I asked God for a second chance. I also asked to be forgiven for my earlier immature and ridiculous response to his invitation.

Sure enough, the same thing happened the next night. I went to sleep only to be awakened in the same manner as the night before. I could sense the Lord giving me an invitation to come and meet with Him. I made my way to the living room and while I could not see Jesus with my physical eyes, the vision of Him sitting in the big chair is still vivid in my mind.

The most accurate way to describe this encounter is to say that it was the closest thing to an actual conversation with Jesus I have ever had. He began by reminding me of a promise that He gave Caryl and me while we were still living in the northwest suburbs of Chicago. He had promised us that when we both turned fifty years old, we would begin to walk together in our destiny and calling and would continue in it for the rest of our lives. In 2008 we both turned fifty. As the Lord was telling me this, I vaguely remembered His promise. How could I have forgotten it? Why hadn't I written it down and start praying it into fulfillment? I don't know why, but I had failed to remember this awesome promise from Heaven. After He reminded me, the memory of it came back. It met a yearning to be all He'd promised for us to be.

I agreed in my spirit and said, "I want what you want for us." I was reminded of Isaiah 6:8, "Then I heard a voice of the Lord saying, 'Whom shall I send? And who will go for us?' And I said, 'Here am I. Send me!'"

Then I asked Him what was in the gold box. In the vision, He opened the box and revealed four keys to me. I stared at the keys for a moment. Then I asked, "What are the keys for?" He said, "These represent the four mandates I'm giving to you and Caryl." Before there was time to formulate my next question, He spoke them in this exact order, "Understanding of the end times, prophetic mentoring, shepherding, and compassion."

I sat in my chair in silence, fear, and awe. It was as if I were frozen in time as the implications of these four mandates began to sink into my soul. I'm not sure how long this lasted, but I began to receive some understanding of what these mandates meant. Let me try to explain.

Understanding The End Times

As I understood the first mandate of "understanding of the end times" it was apparent that I would *not* understand everything there is to know about the subject. I realize this is a hot topic, so, as I write this chapter and mention the end times, I know it will raise questions. It's not as if God were going to somehow download all this understanding to me in an instant and all of a sudden I will become a resident expert on the end times. It almost sounds arrogant or prideful to say that God spoke "understanding of the end times" to me. But He did and I believe. I did have a sense that there might be seasons when He would give me glimpses of His heart on this subject. I'm a bit troubled and puzzled by what this will mean in the future, but I will patiently wait and walk in humility with whatever He decides to share with me.

Prophetic Mentoring

Caryl and I have always wanted to act on everything that is entrusted to us. What good is having something if you can't give it away? The more we get from God, the more eager we are to give it away. Shortly after receiving this revelation or mandate from Heaven, we began a prophetic mentoring small group at The International House Of Prayer (IHOP). It was during this time that the Lord said to me, "Prophetic mentoring is one of the best ideas I ever gave you." That revelation hit me like a ton of bricks. I had always thought prophetic mentoring my own idea. God was gently reminding me that it had been in His heart before He deposited it in mine. I was surprised that the mentoring group began right away; I'm used to waiting several years before God's revelations to me are fulfilled. My human mind naturally thought it would be a several years or more before Caryl and I led a group. God has His own timetable. The group meets at our home, and we encourage others to listen to God for themselves. It is so fun to watch others grow in their giftings.

KEYS TO UNDERSTANDING

Our itinerant ministry, Praiseworthy Ministry, started about fourteen years ago and in the early days, we did a lot of prophetic mentoring. We showed people in small group settings how to listen for the voice of God. Even now, we would much rather teach and minister in small groups or smaller churches than in large conference settings.

Our mentors, Jim and Joyce Gochenour, modeled the method of prophetic mentoring for us. The Lord is allowing us to pass on to others what the Gochenours taught us. It is a privilege to encourage people who desire to grow into their prophetic gift. We are pursuing Corinthians 14:1 for ourselves and for others—to eagerly desire spiritual gifts, especially the gift of prophecy. We love to impart and stir up the gifts in other by the laying on of hands (2 Timothy 1:6). You might be interested in reading *Be Encouraged*, our booklet on prophetic mentoring. You can order it at our website: www.praiseworthyministry.com.

Shepherding

As soon as I heard the word shepherding, I knew it represented the pastoral gifting. Jesus wasn't necessarily telling me that I'd be a pastor or have a church. Shepherding has to do with loving people unconditionally and being tender towards them.

> If I speak in the tongues of men and of angels, but have not love, I am only a resounding gong or a clanging cymbal. If I have the gift of prophecy and can fathom all mysteries and all knowledge, and if I have a faith that can move mountains, but have not love, I am nothing (1 Cor. 13:1-2).

As a shepherd cares for and leads the little lambs, we love and disciple others to lead them to maturity in Christ. We all need to be loved as Jesus loves, and only Christ in us can love rightly. The first commandment is to love Him with all our heart, soul, mind, and strength. The second is to love our neighbors as ourselves (see Mark 12:29-31).

God has opened the door for me to disciple several young men at IHOP. It has been a real blessing to see these young men going hard after God. Some of them need encouragement to get to the next leg of the journey. I am thrilled that God has given me a chance to walk alongside them for a season.

Compassion

I immediately connected and associated with the word compassion. At Metro Christian Fellowship one of the four heart standards was "Compassion for People." Matthew 9:36-38 reads,

> When he saw the crowds, he had compassion on them, because they were harassed and helpless, like sheep without a shepherd. Then he said to his disciples, "The harvest is plentiful but the workers are few. Ask the LORD of the harvest, therefore, to send out workers into his harvest field."

Jesus cared deeply; he was moved by the needs of the people. I believe great victories will come as we put others before ourselves as Jesus does.

The New Shift

Since receiving this life-changing vision, there has been a shift in our lives, and we are trying to discern God's direction for us. I feel as if we are at another launching point, just as I felt before we moved to Missouri. Only God knows what lies ahead, but I believe we have been through a time of God's refining fire and have learned that He is more interested in character and relationship with Him than He is in our giftings.

We've been on quite a journey since leaving our cozy home in Illinois and venturing off to Missouri. When we arrived in Kansas City, our little children were being homeschooled. As I write this last chapter, both our daughters have graduated from college and are married. One is expecting our first grandchild. Our son is now a college senior.

The momentum of many defining and redefining moments carried us to Kansas City, and we feel that each year here has prepared us for the next season. We have learned how to weave a traveling ministry into our family life and receive a regular income from it while we still continued to spend many hours of the day in a quiet lifestyle of prayer. We've also learned how to maintain a lifestyle of prayer during the seasons when God sent us into the marketplace for our income.

Sometimes it has been difficult to figure out when to travel and when to work. At times, Caryl had to take on extra jobs to pay the bills. Some seasons I worked most of the year and found rest and peace in the prayer room after putting in long hours. There has always been an ebb and flow to our life here. Seeking God, keeping current with Him, is a continuing journey that requires flexibility, obedience, and availability. That is what God asked of us fifteen years ago, and we want to continue to follow Him, wherever He leads us. We work for Him.

Caryl and I continue to marvel at His Word and look for Jesus, one day at a time, one encounter at a time, remembering that Jesus never defines success and achievement in houses, cattle, money, or land. Whatever He has for us next, we want to fully embrace it. As we move ahead, we continue to lean on Jesus.

Encouragement

What about you? Has God given you promises that have not yet been fulfilled? Even if they have been years in the making, do not give up.

Are you in the wilderness? (A wilderness is a lonely desolate place, a place of disorder and confusion.) Still waiting patiently (or not so patiently) for God's promises to spring forth? Do not despair or grow tired. **If God led you into the wilderness, He'll surely bring you out. Trust His leadership.** In Matthew 4 and Luke 4 we read that even Jesus was led into the wilderness by the Spirit to be tested. Embrace the wilderness. It will be an opportunity to glorify God. In Luke 4:14, Jesus came out of the wilderness in the power of the Spirit. Looking back on our wilderness experiences, we realize that these were the times when we learned the most.

John the Baptist preached in the wilderness to prepare the way for the Jesus' first coming. Now is the time to prepare the way for Jesus' second coming. Are you willing to go into the wilderness to prepare the way for His return? It may not be fun, but if that is the way for the Lord to refine us and to humble us, it is worth the cost.

Humility is almost always acquired in the desert. (A desert is usually a dry, uncultivated, barren, forsaken, unproductive place.) Moses, David, John the Baptist, and Jesus all had significant training time in the desert. Everyone who is greatly used by the Lord is led into it at some point in their lives.

I'm amused at times when I hear someone say, "God has me in the wilderness. The last three weeks have been really tough on me." If they only knew that it could be years! It was forty for Moses. Sometimes I feel as if the last fifteen years have been a wilderness experience for us.

Maybe you're like us in some ways, ready to be launched into your next season. Are you waiting for the countdown to begin? Are you wondering where your journey will take you? I'm reminded of one of the first Bible verses I memorized:

> **Trust in the LORD with all your heart and lean not on your own understanding; in all your ways acknowledge him, and he will make your paths straight** (Proverbs 3:5).

We all have our God-ordained callings. Each destiny in God is unique. I can't fill the role God has for you, and you can't walk in my divine calling. God's work is tailor-made to fit you perfectly. Over the years, I've heard it preached and found it true in my own life, "God will do His part when we do our part. God can't do His part if we don't do our part."

KEYS TO UNDERSTANDING

We encourage you to take the next step God has for you, your family, or your ministry. As you step out in faith, wait and watch for what God does. It will be a great adventure.

Wholehearted pursuit of your Creator, regardless of the cost, is never a waste of time. A life wasted on Jesus is a life worth living. As you pursue Him, you may not have all the answers for your family and friends, but you need to follow the One who created you. Jesus made one request of His disciples, "Follow Me." Take the next step as God calls you to Himself.

Not that I have already obtained all this, or have already been made perfect, but I press on to take hold of that for which Christ Jesus took hold of me. Brothers, I do not consider myself yet to have taken hold of it. But one thing I do: Forgetting what is behind and straining toward what is ahead, I press on toward the goal to win the prize for which God has called me heavenward in Christ Jesus (Philippians 3:12-14).

Trust Him as you run after Him. It will be worth it!

Afterword

IN LIFE there are certain things that are quite unexplainable. Not to say that our experiences cannot be perceived in a logical categorical order but simply that life will always be filled with questions and second guesses. The intricate webbing that makes up our collective experience is beyond comprehension. In a way, life in itself is faith based (regardless of belief in God). Everything we put our minds to, all of our hopes, fears, shortcomings, and expectations, is based on faith in the fulfillment of our desires and overcoming the obstacles that face us in our lives. For us, the decision our parents made to move to Kansas City is a part of the complicated fabrication of God's sovereign plan for His children. We cannot possibly begin to pretend we understand the plans God had for our family and what is still to come as we continue to grow (in age and maturity in God's larger plan). Although as children we had no direct decision making responsibility for the move to Kansas City, we were being watched closely by our Creator the entire way. With that we will be forever grateful to our parents who loved us and to our heavenly Father who saw our hearts throughout the difficult transition in geographical location and spiritual atmosphere. We rely on our Creator for our individual futures moving forward; through faith we arrived in this city, and through faith we continue our individual journeys. We have learned that we only become free upon realizing that we're not in control of this life. Only when we give our free wills back to our Father in Heaven will we become free in our only true identities, in Christ.

Our family's story has been a life challenge and blessing to all of us. Being a part of our parents' journey while we were children put us in the place of making personal childlike sacrifices of our own. But in the midst of the sacrifices we all made, we are very lucky, blessed, and thankful for Mom and Dad's leadership on how to follow the Lord, no matter what the cost. We have seen them obey what they felt the Lord had called them to do even when it wasn't easy or glamorous!

AFTERWORD

As children, our parents' obedience to follow the Lord placed our lives effortlessly in the will of God, since we were unable to make that decision for ourselves at the time. We know now that this empowered us to overcome challenges in our lives that we would have had to learn to overcome on our own. Our parents have given us the opportunity to know how to hear the Lord for ourselves by modeling it to us every day as we have grown-up. Being a part of our parents' "God Story" has given us the opportunity to walk through the risks, challenges, questions, and personal doubts with the Lord as children protected in the place of not being responsible for anything but our own hearts. This gave us the wisdom we needed before having to do the same thing in our personal lives as responsible adults. This gave us the opportunity to see the blessing and favor of the Lord manifest itself through simple willingness to obey His still small voice.

Now that our family has grown, both in number and in age, we are on our own separate journeys with Lord. We strive to follow the Lord as He speaks differently to each of our hearts—leading us to take risks and steps towards Him that look very different from each other's! The amazing thing about Jesus is that He knows that for one of us it is a sacrifice of obedience to speak (Luke 8:38-39) and to another it is a sacrifice of obedience to be silent (Matthew 9:28-30). Only He knows which will draw us closer to Him (which is the whole point after all)! We've learned that our only requirement is to listen and obey in order to reap the fullness of blessings He has for us.

The story that began with one family has now grown into four different families and stories. We are now all personally accountable to hearing the voice of the Lord for our own life's journeys. We look back and are grateful for learning to hear the voice of the Lord through our parents' knowing that this has lengthened and strengthened our personal relationship with the Lord. Looking back on the few and precious years shared together, as only a family shares, we feel grateful for starting our own journeys with each other. We can now all look back knowing our journeys started in the same place, listening to and obeying the voice of God.

LeAnn, Erin, and Brendan O'Shaughnessy

International House of Prayer: A Forerunner Ministry

WHEN WE MOVED to Kansas City over fifteen years ago and began attending Metro Christian Fellowship, we had no idea that our path as a family would lead us to be part of a forerunner ministry at the International House of Prayer under Mike Bickle.

Let me tell you a little about IHOP. In May 1983, in a very dramatic way, the Lord promised the church leadership at Metro that He would establish a twenty-four-hour-a-day citywide prayer ministry. Sixteen years later, on May 7, 1999, IHOP-KC was officially launched. At IHOP-KC, we are committed to prayer, fasting, the Great Commission, and the forerunner spirit. The work also includes equipping and sending out missionaries as dedicated intercessors and evangelists who work to see revival within the church and a harvest among those searching for God. One of our main mandates is to train believers to love Jesus and others wholeheartedly as they keep the prayer room fire burning and as they go forth to preach the gospel, heal the sick, serve the poor, and plant houses of prayer across the earth.

Let me share the vision statement of IHOP. Hopefully, this will help you get a better understanding of our community in Kansas City.

IHOP-KC Mission and Vision* — We desire:
(1) To call forth, train and mobilize worshipping intercessors who operate in the forerunner spirit as end-time prophetic messengers;
(2) To establish a perpetual solemn assembly in Kansas City by gathering corporately to fast and pray, recognizing this as God's foremost method of establishing justice.
(*http://www.ihop.org/Publisher/Article.aspx?ID=1000043433)

If you would like to learn more about IHOP, the web site is www.ihop.org.

BE ENCOURAGED:
MENTORING AND THE PROPHETIC
by John O'Shaughnessy

In this fast-paced and impersonal culture, people are longing for genuine, loyal relationships—a friend who understands, teaches and cheers us onward. In his new booklet, *Be Encouraged: Mentoring and the Prophetic*, John O'Shaughnessy calls us back to the simple side-by-side relationships that Jesus modeled with his disciples and challenges us to get involved with mentoring others. No matter where you are in your journey of faith, you will benefit immensely from having and being a mentor—it is the essential ingredient necessary for developing prophetic maturity.

ISBN: 978-0-9821835-0-2
To order visit www.praiseworthyministry.com

Prophetic Ministry

If you are interested in having prophetic ministry or prophetic mentoring in your church or small group, please contact us. We'd welcome the opportunity to talk with you in greater detail about tailoring a trip to your personal needs, whether at your location or here in Kansas City.

For additional information, please contact us at:

Praiseworthy Ministry
P.O. Box 461
Grandview, MO 64030

E-mail:
praiseworthyministry@kc.rr.com

Web Site:
www.praiseworthyministry.com

Order Form

Publication	Qty	Price	Total
Keys to Understanding	_____	$10.00	_____
Be Encouraged (booklet)	_____	$4.50	_____

Subtotal: _____

Shipping. Add 20% (minimum $3.00): _____
Tax. (Missouri residents add 7.85%): _____

Total enclosed (U.S. funds only): _____

Your Name: _____

Address: _____

City, State, Zip: _____

E-mail address: _____

Send payment with order to:

Praiseworthy Ministry
P.O. Box 461
Grandview, MO 64030